JAMES BALDWIN

MODERN LITERATURE SERIES

GENERAL EDITOR: Philip Winsor

In the same series:

(continued on last page of book)

JAMES BALDWIN

Carolyn Wedin Sylvander

FREDERICK UNGAR PUBLISHING CO.
NEW YORK

Copyright © 1980 by Frederick Ungar Publishing Co., Inc.
Printed in the United States of America
Design by Anita Duncan

Library of Congress Cataloging in Publication Data

Sylvander, Carolyn Wedin, 1939–
     James Baldwin.

     Bibliography: p.
     Includes index.
     1.   Baldwin, James, 1924–   —Criticism and
interpretation.
PS3552.A45Z9   818′.5409   80–5338
ISBN 0–8044–2484–4
ISBN 0–8044–6891–5 (pbk.)

Contents

Chronology

2 August 1924	Born in Harlem ~~Hospital~~, New York City *to a single mom*
1927	Mother Emma Berdis Jones marries David Baldwin
1930–1935	Attends Public School 24
1935–1938	Attends Frederick Douglass Junior High School
1938	Is converted and preaches (for 3 years) at Fireside Pentecostal Assembly
1938–1942	Attends DeWitt Clinton High School
1940–1941	Contributes to and edits high school literary magazine, *The Magpie*
1942	Graduates from high school, leaves the ministry, takes job with railroad in New Jersey, begins writing *In My Father's House* (to become *Go Tell . . .*)
1943	David Baldwin, stepfather, dies; youngest sister born
1944	Moves to Greenwich Village, meets Richard Wright
1945	Is awarded Eugene Saxton Fellowship with Wright's help
1946	Publishes first book review in *The Nation*
1948	Publishes first essay, "The Harlem Ghetto," and first short story, "Previous Condition," in *Commentary*. Receives Rosenwald Fellowship and leaves for France

1948–1957	Lives in France and Switzerland, briefly returning to the United States in 1952 and 1956
1953	Publishes *Go Tell It on the Mountain*
1954	Receives Guggenheim Fellowship, writes *The Amen Corner*
1955	Publishes *Notes of a Native Son*
1956	*The Amen Corner* is produced at Howard University; publishes *Giovanni's Room,* receives National Institute of Arts and Letters Grant, and *Partisan Review* Fellowship
1957	Returns to the United States, makes first trip to the South
1959	Receives Ford Foundation Grant, returns to France
1960	Returns to United States, travels to the South again to write articles and participate in sit-ins
1961	Publishes *Nobody Knows My Name*
1962	Receives a certificate of recognition from the National Conference of Christians and Jews, publishes *Another Country,* travels to Africa
1963	Publishes *The Fire Next Time,* receives George Polk Memorial Award for magazine articles, becomes nationally known spokesperson on civil rights, is on the cover of *Time* magazine
1964	Publishes *Blues for Mister Charlie,* which opens at ANTA Theatre, Broadway; *The Amen Corner* is professionally produced in Los Angeles; publishes *Nothing Personal* with pictures by Richard Avedon, receives honorary doctor of letters degree from the University of British Columbia, Vancouver, is made member of National Institute of Arts and Letters

1965   Publishes *Going to Meet the Man; The Amen Corner* opens on Broadway and tours Europe

1965   Publishes *The Amen Corner* and *Tell Me How Long the Train's Been Gone*

1971   Publishes *A Rap on Race* (with Margaret Mead)

1972   Publishes *No Name in the Street* and *One Day, When I Was Lost*

1973   Publishes *A Dialogue* (with Nikki Giovanni)

1974   Publishes *If Beale Street Could Talk*

1976   Publishes *The Devil Finds Work* and *Little Man, Little Man,* a children's book, receives an honorary doctor of letters degree from Morehouse College, Atlanta

1979   Publishes *Just Above My Head,* speaks at west coast colleges and universities; is "standing in the wings again, waiting for [his] cue"

Noteworthy Native Son

James Baldwin has been shaped by the age in which he has lived, the turbulent middle years of the twentieth century. He was born in 1924 in a Harlem that was famous, to most of the white Establishment, at least, as the home of Cotton Club Reviews and Josephine Baker and Ethel Waters, blacks who followed the only path blacks could pursue to success at that time—as entertainers. The bitter struggle of his early life—suffering the pain of being black and poor in America, supporting younger brothers and sisters in Harlem, experiencing religious conversion—has yielded brilliant fruit in the passion and humanity of his work.

If most Americans no longer think of Harlem as an incubator for happy jazz entertainers, it is in part due to the wide audience Baldwin reached with *Notes of a Native Son* and *Go Tell It on the Mountain*. If blacks can be seen today as other than entertainers, it is the result of countless successful blacks, not least among whom is Baldwin, who appeared at the right place and at the dramatic time as a young black intellectual symbol. Baldwin reached audiences that had never been reached before by a black artist, and the audiences took Baldwin seriously indeed.

But Baldwin has been not only an artist but an activist. He has criticized passionately the America that he loves. His novels, stories, and essays not only reflect the currents of American life; they have influenced them. James Baldwin has left his mark upon his generation.

Written over thirty-three years, 1947–1980, Baldwin's works form a kind of incremental repetition of nuclear ideas and beliefs. Growth occurs both in an increasingly honest, perceptive, and complete personal look at his childhood and early life and in an increasingly disillusioned attempt to deal honestly, realistically, and positively with the social life of the nation and world around him, with its high hopes and despairing defeats.[1]

Even the briefest summary of Baldwin's biography makes clear the dues he paid—the oppression he faced, the oppression he overcame, and the strength he gained from the battle. Born in Harlem, termed "illegitimate child" in the language of the day, he was followed by eight other children after his mother's marriage to a rigid, white-hating, New Orleans preacher migrated North, the stepfather that Baldwin once said was the only person he ever hated. Baldwin grew up in squalid Harlem tenement surroundings, tending a series of baby brothers and sisters with one hand while turning the pages of a long series of books with the other.

David Baldwin, who married Baldwin's mother in 1927, when James was three years old, became a center of conflict and understanding, hate and respect in Baldwin's early life and in some of his best writing. He is Gabriel Grimes in *Go Tell It on the Mountain;* he is the stepfather whose death and funeral frame the oft-reprinted essay "Notes of a Native Son," first published as "Me and My House" in *Harper's* in 1955. Impossible to get along with, hated by his children while he was alive, David Baldwin nevertheless became for Baldwin emblematic of the pain of being black and male and poor in America. "He had nine children he could hardly feed," Baldwin said in a 1976 inter-

view. "His pain was so great that he translated himself
into silence, rigidity . . . , sometimes into beating us
and finally into madness." [2]

Baldwin describes his mother, Emma Berdis Jones
Baldwin, as "a very tough little woman," [3] both gentle
and strong. " 'You have lots of brothers and sisters,'
she used to say. 'You don't know what's going to happen to them. So you're to treat *everybody* like your
brothers and sisters. Love them.' " [4] It is the last, the
eighth of those brothers and sisters whom Baldwin's
mother gives birth to just a few hours after David
Baldwin's death of a debilitating mental illness in Harlem in 1943, and who serves as the contrasting life-
force in "Notes of a Native Son." The essay develops
with tensions between death and life, hatred and love,
wrong and right stretched tightly between his father's
death, his sister's birth, his own nineteenth birthday and
the Harlem riot of 1943, which seemed a "sustained
and brutally dissonant" coda to mark his father's end
and to correct "the pride of his eldest son," who had
believed, contrary to his father's teachings, that it was
possible to have white friends.[5] In the acceptance of
those tensions, Baldwin finds a balance that encom-
passes the conflicts of his youth and frames his later
artistic activism.

It began to seem that one would have to hold in the mind
forever two ideas which seemed to be in opposition. The
first idea was acceptance, the acceptance, totally without
rancor, of life as it is, and men as they are: in the light of
this idea . . . injustice is a commonplace. . . . The second
idea was of equal power: that one must never, in one's own
life, accept these injustices as commonplace but must fight
them with all one's strength.[6]

The series of baby brothers and sisters young
Baldwin cared for became, in a sense, his salvation
from the Harlem streets. Growing up suffering hateful

mistreatment, entrapment, exploitation, and condescension at the hands of the grocer, the pawnbroker, the butcher, the police, teachers, landlords,[7] beaten by two policemen at age ten,[8] Baldwin found himself, nevertheless, so busy protecting his brothers and sisters "from the rats, roaches, falling plaster, and all the banality of poverty" that he had "no time to go jumping off the roof, or to become a junkie or an alcoholic." "I wanted to become rich and famous," he said, "simply so no one could evict my family again."[9] He explained some of his later speech-making as having its source in growing up as older brother, "telling people what to do and spanking them. . . . In some way I always will be doing that."[10]

The series of books Baldwin read while he tended babies mapped his avenue to fame and riches. By age thirteen, he had read through all the books in the two Harlem libraries and began going downtown to the New York Public Library at 42nd Street.[11] He would later remember Charles Dickens's works, Harriet Stowe's *Uncle Tom's Cabin,* Robert Louis Stevenson's prose and poetry, and Horatio Alger's American rags-to-riches stories as some of his early reading.[12] His debt to American novelist Henry James, whose signed picture Baldwin hung over his work table, was incurred later.[13]

In addition to his family, his Harlem surroundings, and his reading, the other strong influences on Baldwin's early life included his religious conversion, his schooling, and his fascination with the theater. His conversion and ascension at age fourteen to junior preacher at a pentecostal church helped keep him off the streets, probably kept him from admission of his bisexuality, gave him a separate pride to offset his father's repeated reminders of how little and ugly he was, and assured that his later rhetoric would bear an

unmistakable debt to the King James Bible and the
storefront church.

The experience of conversion threads its way
through Baldwin's work, fiction and nonfiction. *Go Tell
It on the Mountain,* his first and best novel, uses a
fictionalized account of the experience as the climax
of the book. In *The Fire Next Time,* Baldwin's famous
1962–1963 book, he tells of the friendships and dangers
that led to the experience, and the doubts and development that led him out of it three years later, to provide
both contrast and premonitory comparison with the
Black Muslims' 1960s impact on the black community.
In *The Devil Finds Work* (1976), Baldwin views that
same conversion and deconversion in terms of his responses to the films and plays he saw before and after
to provide a history of the image of blacks in film. In
each use of the biographical experience, our understanding is enhanced by means of a different viewpoint, context, and intent.

The school experiences and movie and play-
going experiences that provided a countervailing force
to the pentecostal church experience eventually led
Baldwin, at age seventeen, out of the church and out
of Harlem, after his high school graduation in 1942.
The school years were both hard and promising. In
his elementary school years at Public School 24 in
Harlem, "unbelievably shy" Baldwin was called
"Froggy" and "Popeyes." [14] He was inspired, however, by the Negro principal of that school, Mrs. Ayer,
who liked him and who thereby proved "that I was not
necessarily what the country said I was." [15]

A white teacher who encouraged him became for
the young Baldwin "my first key, my first clue that
white people were human," the "first human being to
sort of move out of that kind of monolithic mass that
is composed of the landlords, the pawnbrokers and the

cops who beat you up." [16] In "Notes of a Native Son," Baldwin describes a young white teacher who early encouraged his playwriting by giving him books to read and taking him to the forbidden theatre.

Plotting novels, writing plays, school songs, stories, poetry, Christmas shows throughout elementary and junior high school, at Frederick Douglass Junior High School,[17] Baldwin, by the time he was a sophomore at DeWitt Clinton High School in the Bronx, was co-editor with Richard Avedon of the high school literary magazine, *The Magpie.* "I wasn't a dancer, I wasn't a boxer, I can't sing. And as it turned out I wasn't very good at carrying a mop. So I wrote." [18] In 1964 Baldwin and Avedon, by then a well-known photographer, would again collaborate to create *Nothing Personal,* photographs and text.

By age seventeen, Baldwin had also begun the first of ten years of drafts that would eventually become *Go Tell It on the Mountain.* "In a sense I wrote to redeem my father," he said. "I had to understand the forces, the experience, the life that shaped him before I could grow up myself, before I could become a writer. . . . I became a writer by tearing that book up ·for ten years." [19] Against all the pain and frustration of his father's life and his own life, he early raised his pen: "My revenge, I decided very early, would be to achieve a power which outlasts kingdoms." [20]

Together with school experiences, and the encouragement to his writing those experiences gave, Baldwin's extensive moviegoing did much to lead him from the church in which he was junior minister, from age fourteen to age seventeen, and did much to mold his heroes. In *The Devil Finds Work,* 1976, Baldwin describes his leaving the church as connected with his being taken to the film version of Richard Wright's novel *Native Son* by an American Jewish friend of Spanish descent, who told Baldwin that, if he did not come, "he would be ashamed of me and never speak to me again, and I would be ashamed of myself." [21] The newsreels introduced Baldwin to his first hero, heavyweight boxing champion Joe Louis, and to his first black emperor, Haile Selassie, "pleading vainly with the West to prevent the rape" of Ethiopia.[22]

Leaving home after high school graduation in 1942, Baldwin worked in a series of factories, restaurants, and offices in New Jersey and Greenwich Village, before receiving a Eugene F. Saxton Memorial Trust Fellowship, on black author Richard Wright's recommendation, in 1945. In 1948 he was awarded a Rosenwald Fellowship, as a result of an unpublished book on storefront churches he wrote with Theodore Pelatowski.[23] The Rosenwald Fellowship enabled Baldwin to leave for Paris—as he said, to save his life.

The immediate motivation for Baldwin's 1948 expatriation he later variously described as his decision not to go through with wedding plans—he threw the wedding rings in the Hudson River [24]—and the suicide, in 1964, of a friend with whom he had starved, carried open-housing petitions, and fought landlords. "From the time of this death," Baldwin wrote later, "I began to be afraid of enduring any more. I was afraid that hatred, and the desire for revenge would reach unmanageable proportions in me, and that my end, even if I should not physically die, would be infinitely more horrible than my friend's suicide." [25]

In a broader sense, Baldwin's increasingly frequent departures from and returns to the United States since his first leave-taking on November 11, 1948, result from the difficulty he finds writing in Manhattan. His first leaving was "a devastating shock," but he recognized that "voyagers discover that the world can never be larger than the person that is in the world," [26] and that "there isn't any way ever to leave America." [27]

Europe on little money was indeed full of shocks for Baldwin—from meeting African colonials and discovering he was more American than African or European ("Encounter on the Seine: Black Meets Brown") to encountering Swiss villagers who had never before seen a black person ("Stranger in the Village") to spending Christmas in a Paris jail ("Equal in Paris," all in *Notes of a Native Son*). Shocking, too, was Richard Wright's reaction to Baldwin's criticisms in his 1949 essay, "Everybody's Protest Novel," published in *Zero*, while both Baldwin and Wright were in Paris. Wright felt betrayed by the young writer he had assisted, and their estrangement was permanent. Upon Wright's death, in 1960, Baldwin wrote, "the man I fought so hard and who meant so much to me, is gone." [28] The Baldwin–Wright split on the effectiveness of protest fiction, with Baldwin denying the validity or effectiveness of the kind of verbal protest Wright exemplified, is still an issue among authors and critics of black literature.

In Paris and elsewhere in Europe, Baldwin finished the final version of *Go Tell It on the Mountain,* which was published to excellent reviews in 1953. Briefly returning to New York in 1952, he saw his despised white-liberal acquaintances scrambling to save their skins from Senator Joseph McCarthy's anticommunist lash, and turned to a new art form, in writing the play, *The Amen Corner,* first produced at Howard University, Washington, D.C. in 1954–1955. In demonstration of his other increasingly important art form, eleven of his essays were collected and republished in *Notes of a Native Son* in 1955. In 1957 his second novel, *Giovanni's Room,* appeared, to less favorable reviews, however, than his first novel had received. The subject of *Giovanni's Room,* homosexuality, upset some reviewers and readers.

After receiving a Guggenheim Fellowship in 1954, a *Partisan Review* Fellowship and a National Institute of Arts and Letters Grant in 1956, Baldwin returned to the United States in 1957, to pay more dues in the school-desegregation struggle. His first trip South in 1957 and his many subsequent trips—to interview children braving white taunts and spit, to meet with Congress of Racial Equality (CORE) and student protest leaders, with Medgar Evers, and with Martin Luther King, Jr., to speak to college students, to march, and to attend funerals—testify to the intensity of his involvement with the civil rights effort in the United States. After Baldwin's third, ambitious novel, *Another Country,* appeared in 1962, again to hostile reviews, national attention began to turn toward him as spokesperson for blacks, not as much because of his novels as his essays, debates, interviews, panel discussions.

The galvanizing publication with which Baldwin was to emerge into the spotlight was *The Fire Next Time*, two essays published in book form in 1963 after first appearing in 1962 in *The New Yorker* as "Letter from a Region in my Mind" and in the *Progressive,* "My Dungeon Shook: Letter to my Nephew on the One Hundredth Anniversary of the Emancipation."

The Fire Next Time "created a sensation." The personal, national, and international ideas expressed in it were not particularly new for Baldwin or for the country, but they "brought it all together for a new, influential audience." [29] Baldwin "found himself a celebrity overnight," and "reluctantly, but doggedly, found himself on a whistle-stop speaking tour." [30]

In May of 1963 James Baldwin's portrait was on the cover of *Time* magazine, and, significantly, the article about his speeches, his writing, was not among the book reviews but in the national affairs section.

"Baldwin had made it not as a mere writer, but as an activist, a spokesman," writes William Weatherby in *Squaring Off: Mailer Vs. Baldwin,* a biographical book insightfully summarizing the competing writer-activist roles of Baldwin and Norman Mailer, American novelist and journalist.[31]

As reluctant but dogged spokesperson through the 1960s, Baldwin was rapidly overworked, overtired, and disillusioned. He was finding both frustration and determination in the rapid movement of racial events of the decade, but he needed to retreat to do any writing at all. In May of 1963 he met with Attorney General Robert Kennedy on racial issues, bringing with him not a tame, quiet group of Negro leaders, but friends who "tried to give [Kennedy] an actual experience—the kind of mixed, emotional rap session that was close to the heart of the civil rights movement and the black experience." In December of 1963, in Africa, he was guest of honor at the celebration of Kenya's independence. In 1964 Baldwin was totally involved with the production of his play, *Blues for Mister Charlie,* on Broadway, first getting it into shape for the opening, April 23, then keeping it going. Baldwin left the country to avoid seeing the play close,[32] which it did on August 29, and eventually the play-producing experience led to the fictionalized version of the life of actor Leo Proudhammer in *Tell Me How Long the Train's Been Gone* (1968).

Meanwhile, *Nothing Personal,* with Richard Avedon, was written and published, 1964; a collection of Baldwin's stories, *Going to Meet the Man,* was published in 1965; Baldwin was hired by Columbia Pictures to write a screenplay in Hollywood on the life of Malcolm X (1968); Baldwin appeared before a House of Representatives Select Subcommittee on Labor on establishing a National Commission on Negro History and

Culture; and Baldwin debated everyone from con-
servative William F. Buckley (Baldwin won) to Black
Muslim Malcolm X. The years were filled with interviews, debates, articles, forums, in the United States
and abroad, with serious writing squeeezed in. Awards
and fellowships grew in number. After a Ford Fellowship in 1958, Baldwin received a National Conference
of Christians and Jews Brotherhood Award in 1962;
a George Polk Award, 1963; The Foreign Drama
Critics Award, 1964; an honorary doctor of letters
degree from the University of British Columbia, 1964.
He was made a member of the National Institute of
Arts and Letters in 1964.

And each spring, in the late 1960s, Baldwin says,
"as the weather began to be warmer, my phone would
ring. I would pick it up and find that Washington was
on the line." "Washington" invited Baldwin to lunch,
and "finally, someone would say . . . 'say, Jim. What's
going to happen this summer?' " Baldwin gave the
inevitable litany of needs in the Black ghettoes; inevitably nothing was done, and inevitably summer
brought riots.[33]

The theme of Baldwin's activist and artistic tor-
ment in the 1950s and 1960s lies in the deaths that
shook him personally at their epicenters, while their
reverberations moved around the world. Emmett Till,
the young black man murdered in Mississippi in 1956
whose story was to inspire *Blues for Mister Charlie;*
Medgar Evers, 1963; four little Sunday school girls in
Birmingham, Alabama, 1963 (Baldwin established a
committee to prevent celebrations on Christmas Day
after the bombing) [34]; Malcolm X, 1965; Bobby Kennedy, 1968, who at least *tried,* Baldwin would say;
Martin Luther King, Jr., 1968, two weeks after Baldwin
appeared with him at Carnegie Hall. We know what
suit Baldwin wore to King's funeral, and what hap-

pened to it afterward. In 1972, about King's death, he
would write:

Something has altered in me, something has gone away. Perhaps even more than the death itself, the manner of his
death has forced me into a judgement concerning human
life and human beings which I have always been reluctant
to make.[35]

"I'm the last witness," Baldwin said in 1970 from
Paris. "Everybody else is dead. I couldn't stay in
America, I had to leave." [36] Because of his activism,
Baldwin himself was not and is not free of physical
danger. He made a decision after King's death to leave
the United States, returning only for visits. "I intend
to survive and get my work done." [37]

The 1970s proved quieter for Baldwin, as they
did for the nation he inescapably battled because he
loved it and knew it. The 1971 publication of *A Rap
on Race* with anthropologist Margaret Mead, done
from three long taped conversations between the two,
pulls together some of the knowledge gained through
1960s turmoil and suggests some of the distance Mead
felt that Baldwin had yet to go, to understand world
racism and responsibility. *No Name in the Street,*
Baldwin's most militant essay to date, appeared in
1972. His 1971 taping of a conversation with Nikki
Giovanni, young, black American poet, published
in 1973 as *A Dialogue,* indicates both their differences
and their attempts to understand across generational
boundaries the evolving black liberation movement.
One Day, When I Was Lost, the movie scenario based
on Alex Haley's *Autobiography of Malcolm X,* published rather than filmed, after Baldwin refused to com-
promise with Columbia Pictures on his view of Malcolm's life, also appeared in 1973. Baldwin's novel,
If Beale Street Could Talk, based more on personal
experience with assisting a friend in prison than on the

direct impact of national events, was published in 1974. His unusual autobiographical history of blacks in film, *The Devil Finds Work,* and the children's book using black English and a realistic ghetto setting, *Little Man, Little Man: A Story of Childhood,* were published in 1976.

In contrast to the primacy of Baldwin's public life in the 1960s, Baldwin's personal life comes to the fore in the 1970s. While he was living abroad in Istanbul or outside of Paris much of the time, his visits to the United States were frequently for the purpose of seeing his family and friends, though they also included traveling and lecturing on campuses and other public activity.[38] The black family, father-son relationships, homosexual and heterosexual relationships, the child-preacher, black music and artistry—many of the themes that have occupied Baldwin's personal life appear transformed in his latest novel, *Just Above My Head,* 1979. Baldwin's writing, so voluminous, so diverse, remains a revelation of his life.

From his mature, unfrenetic perspective in the 1970s on the role of the American writer in the political life of the nation, Baldwin does not see retreat, however, but continuing struggle and some hope. In an essay published in 1961, he wrote that "to be an American writer today means mounting an unending attack on all that Americans believe themselves to hold sacred." [39] In an interview twelve years later, Baldwin's view of the American writer had not changed, but it had broadened and deepened.

To try to be a writer (which involves, after all, disturbing the peace) was political, whether one liked it or not. . . . The poet and the people get on generally very badly, and yet they need each other. . . . The poet or the revolutionary is there to articulate the necessity, but until the people themselves apprehend it, nothing happens. . . . An artist is here not to give you answers, but to ask you questions. . . . [Correcting and being corrected by] the role of the artist is exactly the same role, I think, as the role of the lover.[40]

In May of 1976, receiving an honorary doctor of letters degree at Morehouse College, Atlanta, Georgia, Baldwin expressed his belief that, in fact, change had taken place over his lifetime and that the future held hope.

When I was born, blacks generally were born trapped into a white man's fantasy. Black children are not trapped into a white man's fantasy now. . . . I feel a great wheel turning. This has never been a white country and the truth is coming out. Blacks have always been a part of this country but the country was never able to accept that. But we are flesh of the flesh, bone of the bone. And we will triumph.[41]

James Baldwin's life and work will be a significant part of that ultimate triumph.

2

Nonfiction: "One cannot deny
the humanity of another
without diminishing one's own"

What are the nuclear ideas, the beliefs that serve as
centers of development and growth in Baldwin's nonfictional statements, from the book reviews of the
1940s and 1950s to the essays and speeches of the
1960s and the book-length dialogues of the 1970s?

Central to Baldwin's nonfiction is his concept and
use of history. In early book reviews, he outlines the
need for more accurate delineation of the American
past and American pluralism.

Which America will you have? There is America for the
Indians. . . . There is America for the people who settled
the country. . . . There is America for the laborer, for the
financier, America of the North and South, America for the
hillbilly, the urbanite, the farmer. And there is America for
the Protestant, the Catholic, the Jew, the Mexican, the Ori-
ental and that arid sector which we have reserved for the
Negro. These Americans diverge significantly and sometimes
dangerously and they have much in common.[1]

In the early reviews, he also begins to see black
history both as central to black identity and as key to
what must be faced up to in American history.

There is no path out. In a group so pressed down, terrified
and at bay and carrying generations of constricted, sub-
terranean hostility, no real group identification is possible.

Nor is there a Negro tradition to cling to in the sense that
Jews may be said to have a tradition; this was left in Africa
long ago and no-one remembers it now.[2]

The inability to face one's history, as a people or
as a person, means a lack of identity, of maturity.

I believe there is something sleeping beneath the chaos that
is of extraordinary value, if only we have the courage to go
down and bring it up. To destroy, for example, the myth of
the Far West and find out what really happened there; to
destroy the myth of the founding fathers and discover who
they really were, why they came here and what they did.
Because we are the issue of those beginnings, and until we
excavate our history, we will never know who we are.[3]

In order to conquer this continent, the particular aloneness of which I speak—the aloneness in which one discovers
that life is tragic, and therefore unutterably beautiful—could
not be permitted. . . . This continent now is conquered, but
our habits and our fears remain. . . . We know, in the case
of the person, that whoever cannot tell himself the truth
about his past is trapped in it, is immobilized in the prison
of his undiscovered self. This is also true of nations.[4]

On the other hand, accepting "one's past—one's history—is not the same thing as drowning in it, it is
learning how to use it." [5]

In looking at American racial history particularly,
what does one find? On the part of the white oppressor,
whom Baldwin tries desperately to understand, he
sees fear of "the darker side" of life, which fear leads
to creating an external evil to whom fear-releasing
violence can be done. "It has always been much easier
(because it has always seemed much safer) to give a
name to the evil without than to locate the terror
within." [6] On the screaming white faces resisting integration in the South in 1961, he sees fear. "And this
same fear obtains on one level or another, to varying
degrees, throughout the entire country. We would never,

never allow Negroes to starve, to grow bitter, and to die in ghettos all over the country if we were not driven by some nameless fear that has nothing to do with Negroes." [7] White people, Baldwin writes in *The Fire Next Time,* must learn to "accept and love themselves and each other, and when they have achieved this . . . the Negro problem will no longer exist, for it will no longer be needed." [8]

On the part of the black oppressed, without the group identity an accurate history could create, there is rage and self-hate. Baldwin writes of his realization in Europe that he was a "bastard of the West." "I would have to appropriate these white centuries . . . make them mine." He was forced to admit, he writes, that "I hated and feared white people. This did not mean that I loved black people; on the contrary, I despised them, possibly because they failed to produce Rembrandt." [9] "To be a Negro in this country and to be relatively conscious is to be in a rage almost all the time." [10] "There are in this country tremendous reservoirs of bitterness which have never been able to find an outlet, but may find an outlet soon." [11] Baldwin sees the frustration and rage as particularly acute in the black male, whose position is warped by white sexual hang-ups and transfer. "The burden that is placed on you because you're a Negro male is terrifying." [12]

Inescapable in black-white American history is the unity of oppressor and oppressed. This theme is prominent early and late in Baldwin's work. In his 1947 review of Chester Himes's *Lonely Crusader,* "History as Nightmare," he praises the book's value as lying "in its earnest effort to understand the psychology of the oppressed and oppressor and their relationship to each other." [13] And in "Everybody's Protest Novel" he writes that "it must be remembered that the op-pressed and the oppressor are bound together within the same society." [14]

Sometimes in his speeches, Baldwin uses the prison analogy—he is imprisoned in the ghetto, but the man keeping him there, the warden, is to be found in the prison too, and the prisoner knows the warden better than vice versa.[15] Baldwin's most commonly quoted statement of this theme is in "Fifth Avenue, Uptown," *Nobody Knows My Name,* 1961. "It is a terrible, an inexorable, law that one cannot deny the humanity of another without diminishing one's own: in the face of one's victim, one sees oneself." [16]

But it is the unity of white and black in oppression that contains some promise for America. In the passage Baldwin chooses to place at the end of *Notes of a Native Son,* in "Stranger in the Village," he contrasts the "warp and woof of the heritage of the West, the idea of white supremacy," with his *not* being "a stranger any longer for any white American alive. . . . It is precisely this black-white experience which may prove of indispensable value to us in the world we face today. This world is white no longer, and it will never be white again." [17] At some point in the rage and frustration of oppression, "you realize that your suffering does not isolate you; your suffering is your bridge." [18]

Early, Baldwin draws a contrast between integration and assimilation. Integration necessitates equally valued cultural knowledge and exchange; an assimilated culture loses its distinguishing features. Integration doesn't mean giving me something, he repeats frequently, it means "the country will have to turn and take me in its arms." For example, "when the church . . . embraces all Christians, the church will have had to change." [19] "I am not a ward of America, I am not an object of mission and charity, I am one of the people who built the country." [20] One of the values of desegregation of public facilities, he said, is to "make white people get used to seeing you around without a broom in your hand. . . . The wall has been built on every single level and has got to come down on every level." [21] The word integration means, if anything, that "we with love, shall force our brothers to see themselves as they are, to cease fleeing from reality and begin to change it." [22] On the riots of 1965 and following, he asks, "Who is looting whom? . . . You're accusing a captive population who has been robbed of *everything* of looting. I think it's obscene. . . . He doesn't want [the TV set]. He wants to let you know he's there." [23] Viewing the whole civil rights movement retrospectively, Baldwin says that it revealed a "profound hostility . . . on the part of a whole lot of black people, old and young. . . . It was a passionate example. It was doomed to political failure, but that doesn't make any difference." [24]

All along, Baldwin has recognized the difficulty of change, for "any real change implies the breakup of the world as one has always known it, the loss of all that gave one an identity, the end of safety." [25] Even the oppressed, finally, resist change. There is "something unutterably painful about the end of oppression . . . and one flinches from the responsibility, which we all now face, of judging black people solely as people." [26] The oppressed "have become in some sense accustomed to their oppression. I don't mean that they accept it or that they like it, but they *know* it." [27]

The difficulty for the reformer, the activist, is in remaining in touch with the people he or she has acted for.

Perhaps the worst thing that can be said about social indignation is that it so frequently leads to the death of personal humility. Once that has happened, one has ceased to live in that world of men which one is striving so mightily to make over. One has entered into a dialogue with that terrifying deity, sometimes called History, previously, and perhaps again, to be referred to as God, to which no sacrifice in human suffering is too great.[28]

⋆Though politically Baldwin speaks for the necessity of a third party [29] and of the inevitability of decentralization and socialism,[30] he maintains a distance from theories and ideologies. In 1955, he states, "I think all theories are suspect, that the finest principles may have to be modified, or may even be pulverized by the demands of life, and that one must find, therefore, one's own moral center. . . ." [31] After his pulverization by the demands of the 1960s, Baldwin says, in 1972,

I don't have any coherent political ideology—nothing very doctrinaire. I know more clearly what I'm against than I can state what I'm for. . . . There's something about me which mistrusts that level of political indoctrination. . . . The danger of trying to indoctrinate a population is that you then cease to listen to them.[32]

As to his own role, Baldwin is clear on the conflicts and challenges it continuously involves.

Writers are extremely important in a country, whether or not the country knows it. The multiple truths about a people are revealed by that people's artists—that is what the artists are for. . . . Societies are never able to examine, to overhaul themselves; this effort must be made by that yeast which every society cunningly and unfailingly secretes. This ferment, this disturbance, is the responsibility, and the necessity, of writers.[33]

The difficulty, for the activist writer, is resisting simplification. Because of rage, there is a "great temptation to simplify the issues under the illusion that if you simplify them enough, people will recognize them. . . . As a writer, you have to decide that what is really important is not that the people you write about are Negroes, but that they are people, and that the suffering

of any person is really universal." [34] And again, after
the 1960s, he repeats the need to resist simplification.

The hardest thing [the artist] has to do is to remain an artist. . . . I have to do what I can do and bear witness to
something that has to be there when the battle is over. . . .
You have to speak in slogans when you are in the middle of
our situation. And yet you got to be aware that a slogan is
only a slogan. . . . What you have to do is insist on complexity which people in the battle don't want to think about.[35]

Baldwin seems to sum up the role he sees for himself as
"witness." He is no longer exactly of the people he
writes of, jetting around the world as he does, but he
sees himself as a witness. "That's my responsibility. I
write it all down." What is the difference, then, of an
observer and a witness? "An observer has no passion.
It doesn't mean I saw it. It means I was there." [36] The
responsibility is to the future: "We are meant to be
witnesses to a possibility which we will not live to see,
but we have to bring it out." [37]

And yet James Baldwin is in many ways *of* the
people he writes of and speaks of. The closeness he
feels to, and the responsibility he feels for, his family,
germinated back in the days when he took responsibility for the series of babies his mother inexplicably
brought home from the hospital, now expresses itself
in concern for his profusion of nieces and nephews.
"The most important thing for me is how to save our
children. They only have us to do that. . . . One can
change the situation, even though it may seem impossible. But it must happen inside you first." [38]

It is appropriate to end a survey of the nuclear
ideas of Baldwin's nonfiction with a concept, a word,
he often uses but which is often misunderstood or mis-
read. The word is "love." His use of the term comes
directly out of his experience. About his large and

conflict-ridden Harlem family, he says, "if we had not loved each other, none of us would have survived." [39] About his personal experience in finding love, he writes that "because you love one human being, you see everyone else very differently than you saw them before . . . and you are both stronger and more vulnerable." [40] About his country, which he says he can never leave, no matter how much he lives abroad, he writes "I love America more than any other country in the world, and, exactly for this reason, I insist on the right to criticize her perpetually." [41] In attempting to explain what he means when he says "I believe in love," he writes:

I don't mean anything passive. I mean something active, something more like a fire, like the wind, something which can change you. I mean energy. I mean a passionate belief, a passionate knowledge of what a human being can do, and become, what a human being can do to change the world in which he finds himself. [42]

Baldwin's *Dialogue* with Nikki Giovanni ends with Giovanni saying, "Love is a tremendous responsibility," and Baldwin responding, "It's the only one to take, there isn't any other." [43]

The form in which Baldwin writes nonfiction—and often speaks—is dependent for its impact and memorability on rhetorical devices he uses skillfully and repeatedly. The metaphoric comparisons are clever and apt. An anthology, he says in a 1948 book review, "appeals to me usually about as strongly as watered whiskey; but, of course, your watered whiskey is better than none." [44] In another review that year, he describes an author as, "when not downright revolting, obscurely and insistently embarrassing. Not only did he have nothing to say, but he drooled, so to speak, as he said it." [45] About expatriate activities in Paris from 1946 on, he says that "magazines were popping up like toadstools and vanishing like fog." [46] Artists, "if they are to survive," he says, "are forced, at last, to tell the whole story, to vomit the anguish up." [47]

The fitting phrase or image can be seen in Baldwin's description of men he knew. He describes author Norman Mailer through others' distant discussions: "And people yelled about Norman with a kind of avid glee, which I found very ugly. Pleasure made their saliva flow, they sprayed and all but drooled, and their eyes shone with that blood-lust which is the only real tribute the mediocre are capable of bringing to the extraordinary." [48] Baldwin describes famed Swedish film and stage director Ingmar Bergman as "a tall man, economically, intimidatingly lean," "there being about him the evangelical distance of someone possessed by a vision." [49] And about Martin Luther King, Jr., Baldwin expresses wonder as to what "complex of miracles" prepared him for where he stood in the 1961 Civil Rights Movement.[50]

Parallelism in phrasing and in sentence structure, together with repetition of words, are common Baldwin patterns. About his youth, he says "you were not expected to aspire to excellence. You were expected to make peace with mediocrity." [51] "The American way of life," he says, "has failed—to make people happier or to make them better. We do not want to admit this, and we do not admit it." [52]

It is, however, particularly in the autobiographical base for the essay that Baldwin has been distinctive in his nonfictional writing. The essays, except for titles, are not usually revised much as they are gathered from periodicals and reprinted in collected form— short, journalistic paragraphs may be combined, a few sentences or paragraphs may be deleted or added, emphasis may be changed with elimination of italics.[53] Some essays, of course, have not ever appeared in collected form—the reader must go to *Mademoiselle*

magazine of August, 1960, for example, for the powerful chronologically-based, journalistic piece on the
early Civil Rights Movement in the South, "They Can't
Turn Back."

In the best of his essays, collected or uncollected,
it is Baldwin's insightful and honest use of his own
history that serves to generate, develop, and sustain
his ideas. By taking the reader through the experiences
that led to thoughts or feelings, he brings him to
a clear understanding of, if not belief in, the ideas.
"Down at the Cross," in *A Fire Next Time,* opens with
fourteen-year-old Harlem boys and girls on the avenue
at "the beginning of our burning time." From daily
humiliation and danger, "the wages of sin . . . visible
everywhere," Baldwin flees to the church, "my gim-
mick." It is his gradual discovery of lack of love in the
Christian church ("It was a mask for hatred and self-
hatred and despair"), that leads the essay into his later
adult encounter with Elijah Muhammad, leader of the
Black Muslims. Out of the contrasts and similarities
between the Christian injunction to wash your sins and
be whiter than snow and the Black Muslim insistence
that the white man is the devil come Baldwin's syn-
thesis and warning. We must have honesty, love, integration; we must learn from the past. If we do not,
the Old Testament warning, "created . . . in song by
a slave," from which the book takes its title, is clear:
*"God gave Noah the rainbow sign, No more water,
the fire next time!"*

The organization of the Baldwin essay so inten-
sively using personal experience is not always chronological. "Fifth Avenue Uptown: A Letter from Harlem," is essentially spatial in order, moving from the
housing project now standing where Baldwin's youthful
home stood, out to the streets surrounding, into the
city and nation and world in contrast, and back to the
hated housing project. "Walk through the streets of

Harlem," the essay concludes, "and see what we, this nation, have become."

Two lesser known, but powerful essays do again, however, use a chronological order to convey idea out of experience. "Stranger in the Village" begins with Baldwin's experience of being the only black face ever seen in the tiny Swiss village in which he finished writing *Go Tell It on the Mountain* and moves to an analysis of his exclusion from the cultural history of western civilization. The essay does for Baldwin's view of his larger cultural history what the better-known "Notes of a Native Son" does for his personal, family, and American history, with both essays following a repeated experience-to-idea plan. "Equal in Paris," a second lesser-known essay, is based on the humorous but terrifying experience of being imprisoned eight days over Christmas, 1949, for a stolen bed sheet borrowed from an American friend who had taken it from a hotel. Through self-mocking, close description of the sequence of events, Baldwin takes the reader with him to an understanding of Parisian character, Parisian (and American) justice, negative and positive aspects of "culture," and "the laughter of those who consider themselves to be at a safe remove from all the wretched." "I had not known," he says of imprisonment, "that when one's shoelaces and belt have been removed one is, in the strangest way, demoralized. The necessity of shuffling and the necessity of holding up one's trousers with one hand turn one into a rag doll." [54]

Baldwin essays that do not use the intense personal experience as base are often weaker, less memorable, and less convincing than those that do. An essay like "A Question of Identity," on the American student colony in Paris, or the two essays that are remembered for their criticism of Richard Wright, "Everybody's Protest Novel," and "Many Thousands

Gone," seem pretentious, lacking in personality, partly because they appear to be generalizing from experience without concomitant honesty and directness about the experience.

Baldwin's essays effectively use traditional rhetorical devices of metaphor, parallelism, repetition, and develop a characteristic autobiographical, organic growth from experience to idea. Robert Sayre has said of current autobiographies by those whose ancestors were not "within the pale of 'civilization' as the earlier generation recognized it"—blacks, women—that "they have extended concepts of self and of society at the same time. They have made their personal dreams and nightmares a part of the public discourse. Rather than consult the statistics and opinion surveys, they have counseled with their own pasts and personal needs." [55]

James Baldwin has counseled with his past thoroughly and honestly, and his past has been part of the largest issues to face the United States and the rest of the world in the twentieth century—poverty, race, sex, power, change. Three words that describe James Baldwin's nonfiction are "honest," "realistic," and "life-giving." Students of cultural and social history would do well to listen very closely to this exceedingly articulate witness.

3

"I'm ready," "I'm coming," "I'm on my way": *Go Tell It on the Mountain*

Go Tell It on the Mountain opens on the fourteenth birthday of John Grimes, in the Harlem tenement in which he lives with his parents, younger brother, Roy, and two younger sisters, Sarah and Ruth.[1] The epigraph for Part I, "The Seventh Day," reads "I looked down the line, / And I wondered." And indeed John Grimes on his fourteenth birthday wonders. He wonders about everyone always saying he will be a preacher, like his father, and he has even "come to believe it himself." He wonders about his mother's expecting another child; from earliest memory, he has feared her swelling belly, "knowing that each time the swelling began it would not end until she was taken from him, to come back with a stranger."

He wonders about the Saturday night "sinners" along the avenue as the cleaned-up Grimes family walk to church on Sunday mornings. He wonders about the sexual activities visible in basements and hallways, and about his mother and father doing "it," too, "over the sounds of rats' feet, and rat screams, and the music and cursing from the harlot's house downstairs."

In the Temple of the Fire Baptized, John wonders about Elisha, the pastor's seventeen-year-old nephew, who "was already saved and a preacher." He wonders about his brother Roy, whom no one expects to be good, to learn his Sunday school lesson, or to grow up to be a preacher. He wonders about the power of the singing, shouting, and dancing of the Sunday morning services, "as though wherever [the saints] might be became the upper room, and the Holy Ghost were riding on the air." Most of all, he wonders about his father, Gabriel, whose "awful" face becomes "more awful" under the power of the pentecostal service, whose "daily anger" is "transformed into prophetic wrath."

On his fourteenth birthday, John Grimes awakens worrying about the sin of his sexual experimentation and thought, but determined to move out from "the darkness of his father's house . . . and his father's church," to "where he would eat good food, and wear fine clothes, and go to the movies as often as he wished." His means will be his intelligence, his schooling, like a shield if not a weapon against his father's hatred, beatings, restrictions, and self-righteousness.

He listens as his mother and Roy argue, as his mother defends Gabriel—"Your Daddy beats you . . . because he loves you"—and he does his Saturday morning chore of sweeping the faded front-room carpet, with dust "clogging his nose and sticking to his sweaty skin." He dusts the old photographs of his brother and sisters, his mother and father and his aunt Florence, and his own, the naked figure, showing him lying on a white counterpane.

When John's mother gives him his birthday present, a few coins from a bright vase, he heads across Central Park to Fifth Avenue downtown, where he samples imaginatively the world of food, clothes, movies, books, and wealth outside his Harlem prison. His return home, however, is like "the beginning of the fulfillment of a prophecy," for Roy has been cut up in a fight with white boys, "the white folk *you* like so much," Gabriel sneers at John. Gabriel's excessive concern for Roy is transformed into his slapping his wife for not caring for the children properly and then into his beating Roy with a belt as Roy defends his mother. Aunt Florence, visiting the family, concludes the scene with a judgement of Gabriel: "You was born wild, and you's going to die wild. But ain't no use to try to take the whole world with you. You can't change nothing, Gabriel. You ought to know that by now."

John, from whose third-person, limited omniscient point of view Part I of *Go Tell It on the Mountain* is told, does not know what Florence knows, does not know, except vaguely, Florence's past or Gabriel's past or his mother's past. But as Part I concludes, with John and Elisha readying the church for the Saturday night Tarry Service and with the arrival of Florence, Gabriel, and Elizabeth, John's mother, at the church door, the reader is lead into a revelation not shared with fourteen-year-old John. That revelation comes in Part II, "The Prayers of the Saints," with "Florence's Prayer," "Gabriel's Prayer," and "Elizabeth's Prayer" told in the third-person, limited point of view from each of those characters in turn. Only occasionally in Part II are we brought back to the present and to John, as we learn of the individual and collective histories that have such impact on him.

Aunt Florence's arrival at church surprises John. "She had never entered this church before." As her "prayer" begins, we discover her reason for being there now—she is dying. Every night brings death "a little closer to her bed." And she is terrified. "The message had come to Florence that had come to Hezekiah: *Set thine house in order, for thou shalt die and not live.*" The epigraph for Florence's prayer, from the Charles Wesley Christmas song, "Hark the Herald Angels Sing," is "Light and life to all he brings / Risen with healing in his wings."

Florence's memory moves back to her youth in the South, to the indelible scene in a dark, barricaded

house, of her mother's prayers for protection after another black girl, Deborah, has been gang-raped by
white men. It is "the first prayer Florence heard, the
only prayer she was ever to hear in which her mother
demanded the protection of God more passionately
for her daughter than she demanded it for her son."
For Florence's young frustration is with the double
standard imposed on her after Gabriel's birth. "There
was only one future in that house" run by her deserted
mother, "and it was Gabriel's—to which, since Gabriel was a manchild, all else must be sacrificed."

Florence's rebellion culminates in leaving home
under her mother's deathbed curse, to go North, never
to return. In the North, she falls in love with and
marries Frank, struggling with submission to love and
sex, submission to Frank's less ambitious and less respectable life-style. Frank suffers from her frustrated
ambitions and after ten years leaves her. He dies later
in France in World War I. "But it had been from the
first her great mistake—to meet him, to marry him, to
love him as she so bitterly had. Looking at his face,
it sometimes came to her that all women had been
cursed from the cradle; all, in one fashion or another,
being given the cruel destiny, born to suffer the weight
of men." Now, later still and near death, after years of
surviving by mopping floors, Florence finds no light or
life or healing in the Temple of the Fire Baptized. She
can think only of revenge against her brother Gabriel.
She carries in her purse a letter from Gabriel's previous
wife, her raped childhood friend, Deborah, which
might provide that revenge, by revealing to Elizabeth
Gabriel's past sin. Florence "had always thought of this
letter as an instrument in her hands which could be used
to complete her brother's destruction." But now God
was to strike her, not her brother, down. "The hands
of death caressed her shoulders, the voice whispered
and whispered in her ear: 'God's got your number,

knows where you live, death's got a warrant out for you.' "

"Gabriel's Prayer," the second of the three "Prayers of the Saints" in Part II of *Go Tell It on the Mountain,* forms the structural center of the novel. His epigraph is "Now I been introduced / To the Father and the Son, / And I ain't / No stranger now." As Gabriel's story is told through his memory, it is clear that "Father" and "Son" refer not only to God and Jesus Christ, but to the sons Gabriel fathers and rejects, adopts and hates, fathers and finds disappointing.

The young Gabriel's story begins with his older sister Florence's abrupt departure from their mother's house, with their mother abed, lingering only in order to see Gabriel "saved" before she dies. Gabriel is a wastrel—spending his money, time, and seed on drink and loose women. But eventually he no longer can hold back against his mother's prayers, and his own disgust and fear. He is saved under a tree, returning home early one morning.

And, yes, there was singing everywhere; the birds and the crickets and the frogs rejoiced, the distant dogs leaping and sobbing, circled in their narrow yards, and roosters cried from every high fence that here was a new beginning, a blood-washed day! And this was the beginning of his life as a man.

In short order Gabriel turns to preaching and marries bony Deborah, who has emerged from her childhood shame of rape "like a woman mysteriously visited by God, like a terrible example of humility, or like a holy fool." Gabriel's guidance toward this marriage comes from two dreams. The first, a wet dream, signifies to him that world of women and sin and Satan he must battle to stay clear of. The other dream, of climbing a high mountain, attaining a peaceful field from which "the elect" are seen toiling upward, represents to him a promise. " 'So shall thy seed be,' " a voice says before he wakes.

But holy Deborah, alas, is barren and permanently damaged in her sexuality by the gang-rape of her youth. Deborah and Gabriel's joyless marriage bed makes Gabriel vulnerable to the appeal of a young girl, Esther, who works for the same white family he does. In their nine-day affair, Esther conceives, and when later she tells him of her pregnancy, he takes money from Deborah to send Esther north to Chicago. Esther dies in childbirth, living long enough only to name her son (Gabriel's firstborn but unclaimed son) "Royal," mocking Gabriel's claim that his son would be a royal line, a royal child, in the line of the faithful. Royal grows to manhood in his grandparents' home, before Gabriel's eyes. It is only after Royal is dead in a bar fight back in Chicago that Gabriel admits to Deborah what she has known all along, that Royal was his son. " 'But Gabriel,' " she says, " 'if you'd said something even when that poor girl was buried . . . I wouldn't nohow of cared what folks said, or where we might of had to go, or nothing. I'd have raised him like my own,—and he might be living now.' "

After Deborah's death and Gabriel's move North, he seems to have a chance to redeem himself in the personages of Elizabeth, who comes forward to the altar one night as he preaches, and her fatherless son, John. But John, the unwitting stepchild, is followed by another Royal, Gabriel's blood-son by Elizabeth, and John can find no favor in his stepfather's eyes. As Roy, the true son, fights, misbehaves, curses his father, John, the stepson, acts out all the roles of righteousness Gabriel covets for Roy. And John, too, hates Gabriel—"in the very grave he would hate him." Gabriel's "prayer," the central section of the book, ends with Gabriel ordering John to " 'kneel down,' " and with

John turning suddenly, "the movement like a curse," to kneel before the altar.

The final prayer of the saints belongs to Elizabeth, John's mother. "Lord, I wish I had of died / In Egypt land!" is the appropriate epigraph for her story of love and tragedy. Elizabeth's beautiful, light-skinned mother dies when Elizabeth is eight, "an event not immediately recognized by Elizabeth as a disaster," since her mother had lavished little love or attention on her—as Elizabeth suspected—because "she was so very much darker than her mother and not nearly, of course, so beautiful." Being taken away from her father to live with an aunt is the real disaster, for her father is "dark, like Elizabeth, and gentle, and proud," although he runs a house of prostitution.

Elizabeth grows up determined to escape her aunt's house, much as her son John later determines to escape Gabriel's. The escape comes in the form of a brilliant and bitter young man, Richard, who takes her "out of that house, and out of the South, and into the city of destruction." Her love for Richard is boundless, but the conditions under which they live separately in Harlem, without promised marriage, are not reassuring. Their brief happy times end with Richard's being falsely charged with robbery. Despite ultimate acquittal, Richard has been beaten, shamed, and defeated. He slashes his wrists and dies in blood-soaked sheets, and Elizabeth berates herself for not telling him of her pregnancy, which might have given him determination to continue his battles.

When Elizabeth and Richard's John is six months old, she meets and becomes friends with Florence, while both work cleaning a Wall Street office building. Through Florence, she meets Gabriel, just come North, who appears, "in Florence's tiny, fragile, parlor a very rock . . . in [Elizabeth's] so weary land." Now, in the present time of the novel, with John fourteen and with three other children, Elizabeth thinks back on Gabriel's broken promise to love her firstborn, and on John's birth, "the beginning of her life and death." As his cry pierced through her pain on the day of his lonely birth, so "now in the sudden silence" of the Temple of the Fire Baptized, "she heard him cry: not the cry of the child, newborn . . . but the cry of the man-child, bestial, before the light that comes down from heaven." Here, at the end of Part II of *Go Tell It on the Mountain,* with Gabriel staring "struck rigid as a pillar in the temple," lies John "on the threshing-floor, in the center of the crying, singing saints, . . . astonished beneath the power of the Lord."

Part III returns us full force to the consciousness of young John Grimes as he lies astonished. "Then I buckled my shoes, / And I started" reads the epigraph for his experience of conversion. Dust fills his nostrils and mouth here as it did in the morning as he swept the carpet, but the voice that tells him to "leave this temple and go out into the world" is now powerless to raise him.

As the prayers, songs, stamping of feet, and dancing of the saints vibrate around and over him, we see, hear, smell, taste them all through John's astonished consciousness. The depth and the darkness he must endure are peopled by his father's curse above all, by his vision of his father's nakedness, by "the despised and rejected, the wretched and the spat upon, the earth's offscouring."

At the turning point, as John cries "Lord, have mercy," a voice comes through "the rage and weeping, and fire, and darkness and flood." The voice is Elisha's: " 'Go through. Go through.' " And at the culminating moment of vision and delight, it is again Elisha's voice that comes to John through his tears:

" 'Oh, yes! . . . Bless our God forever!' " For John "the light and the darkness had kissed each other, and were married now, forever, in the life and the vision of John's soul."

As the praying saints lift him to his feet and congratulate him, it is Gabriel's song that is sung: "Lord, I been introduced to the Father and the Son, / And I ain't / No stranger now!" And now, against Gabriel, John has some defense and some revenge. To the father who does not touch him, kiss him, or smile at him, he responds shakily, " 'I'm going to pray God . . . to keep me, and make me strong . . . to stand . . . to stand against the enemy . . . and against everything and everybody . . . that wants to cut down my soul.' "

As the saints leave the church, "the filthy streets [ring] with the early-morning light." As they walk along the avenue, the gutters flow with "paper, burnt matches, sodden cigarette-ends; gobs of spittle, green-yellow, brown, and pearly; the leavings of a dog, the vomit of a drunken man, the dead sperm, trapped in rubber, of one abandoned to his lust."

But temporarily, it is all washed clean and bright with joy for John, as he and Elisha walk first of the three groups going home from the Tarry Service. Behind them come Gabriel and Florence, with Florence, after thirty years, revealing to Gabriel her knowledge of his past life with Esther and Royal, vowing not to die in silence. " 'It'll make Elizabeth to know . . . that she ain't the only sinner in your holy house. And little Johnny, there—he'll know he ain't the only bastard.' " And further behind yet walk Elizabeth, Sister McCandless, Sister Price, and Praying Mother Washington, with Elizabeth thinking, irredeemably, of Richard.

At the Grimes's door, Elisha kisses John on the forehead, "a holy kiss . . . like a seal ineffaceable forever." At the same time, John feels his father behind him and the March wind on his damp clothing. He turns to face his father, who does not smile.

They looked at each other a moment. His mother stood in the doorway, in the long shadows of the hall.
"I'm ready," John said, "I'm coming. I'm on my way."

So ends *Go Tell It on the Mountain*.

The overall structure of this first and rather short Baldwin novel (running 221 pages in the Dell paperback edition) is skillfully controlled and manipulated to convey an important point, which we have seen also in his essays. That point is the impact of history—personal and collective—on an individual, whether or not that individual is aware of the history. Michel Fabre has aptly compared the structure of *Go Tell It on the Mountain* to a triptych, with John's story the side panels and the central panel giving "the converging stories" of Florence, Gabriel, and Elizabeth. Gabriel, dominant center of the center panel, "usurps first place. The son is dispossessed of his story by the fate of his father." [2] John Grimes's consciousness controls Part I, fifty pages, and Part III, twenty-nine pages; almost twice that space is devoted to those whose experiences control the events of John's young life.

Gabriel's past, furthest structurally from John's portion of the novel, is also the least known and the most difficult for John. Were Florence to make some of Gabriel's past known to John, as she threatens to do at the end of the novel, John could be released from the hatred and need he feels for Gabriel. Were John to know that Gabriel is not his true father, he could understand the hatred directed toward him. Were John to know of Gabriel's past affair with Esther and of his unclaimed, dead firstborn son, he could, perhaps, see his stepfather as both more sinful and more human. But John does not know. The physical, psychological, spiritual struggles that have made Gabriel the hard, self-righteous, violent man that he is in Harlem in the 1930s are all unknown to John.

Similarly, if less violently, the distance John at times feels from his mother, as though she is thinking and feeling and knowing much more than she is saying or revealing, might be lessened were John aware of her youthful love for Richard and of Richard's suicide. Elizabeth at times sees Richard in their son, John. But the intelligence that is one part of John's inheritance from his real father will have tough going against the weakness and despair that is also a part of that inheritance, unless John has some awareness of that dangerous weakness and some weapon against it.

It is painfully, dramatically, structurally clear throughout *Go Tell It on the Mountain* that the struggles every individual faces—with sexuality, with guilt, with pain, with love—are passed on, generation to generation. Whether or not a fourteen-year-old knows or senses them, experiences of his mother and father years before move his own world.

When one moves from the impact of the personal past of his stepfather and father and mother on John to the impact of a collective past, it is useful to consider Florence's story as suggesting some of that larger history. Florence is the only character of *Go Tell It on the Mountain* without a Biblical name and the only primary character who essentially rejects the protection and survival mechanism of religion as a way of life and denial of life. She leaves her mother on her deathbed, despite the supernatural fear such an act induces; she works out her physical survival without aid of the church; her ambitions and goals of respectability and economic well-being are nonspiritual. Even up against death, though she tries the Temple of the Fire Baptised for comfort, she does not give in to religious ecstasy nor achieve religious solace. Instead she determines to leave a witness after her death that is essentially just, not merciful, unforgiving, even revengeful—Deborah's thirty-year-old letter.

Florence's experience represents a double group-discrimination. She suffers socially, economically, physically because of her color—hence her bleaching creams, her urges toward respectable behavior. She suffers also because of her sex. From the vulnerability of female anatomy and sexuality made clear in both the violent rape of Deborah and in Frank's dominance in the bedroom to the educational discrimination of her mother's giving Gabriel the schooling he wastes and Florence so badly wants, she has suffered from being female.

Florence is perhaps the strongest character psychologically in the novel. She has not taken the escape route of religion, nor has she fallen into the secular escapism of drink or drugs or dependency. But there is little comfort or joy in her life and little hope as she faces death. She knows only enough and has only enough power to possibly relieve some of Elizabeth's and John's future pain in dealing with Gabriel. That power, however, is slightly more power than any of the other characters have.

Florence's move from the rural South to the urban North is emblematic of the great migration of Negroes from South to North in the second decade of the century. One of the unacknowledged tensions John Grimes is dealing with is that incomplete adjustment to the Northern mores, Northern cadences, Northern habits by his aunt, mother, and stepfather, all of whose lives begin in the South. Florence's move North is the most deliberate and conscious, and Florence also comes closest to adjusting without having to retain the umbilical cord of essentially Southern religious fundamentalism.

While the collective history of blacks in America is perhaps clearest in Florence's story, it must be emphasized that the national cancer of virulent white racism, while not explicitly and continually exposed in the novel, is nevertheless the underlying tissue-culture of all the characters' lives. One example will illustrate the underlying racism. In Gabriel's prayer we find that his one brief conversation with his son Royal occurs as these two black men meet on a corner in the "dark and silent town" paralyzed by "death and destruction," "where white men prowled like lions," after the body of a black soldier is found.

The soldier's "uniform [is] shredded where he had been flogged"; "he lay face downward at the base of a tree"; when he is turned over, "his eyeballs stared upward in amazement and horror, his mouth was locked open wide; his trousers, soaked with blood, were torn open, and exposed to the cold, white air of morning, the thick hairs of his groin, matted together, black and rust-red."

The reader may recall that in the United States between 1882 and 1927 there were 3,513 known lynchings. Over seventy blacks were lynched in 1919 alone, ten of them soldiers, some still in uniform. Fourteen were burned publicly, eleven while still alive.[3] Gabriel, in *Go Tell It on the Mountain,* can walk the streets after the murder only because he is a preacher, and he must walk with his head bowed. His warning to Royal to be careful is only temporarily effective. Eventually Royal is killed in the kind of male-threatening violence that Gabriel escapes through the church —through being a "good," and sex-less, "nigger."

The danger of black male sexuality and power as well as black female helplessness against white power are of course part of the collective inheritance John Grimes is unwittingly struggling with on his fourteenth birthday. Just as his relatives' personal histories are unknown to him, so, too, is this collective history hidden. In 1935, the year in which this novel is set, United States history books called the killing of seven men at

Boston, Massachusetts, in 1770 "The Boston Massacre," but those same books did not mention lynchings. In his personal and his collective history, then, John Grimes is held in that limbo of blind identity-seeking that Baldwin describes in the essay "Creative Dilemma" in 1964: "We know, in the case of the person, that whoever cannot tell himself the truth about his past is trapped in it, is immobilized in the prison of his undiscovered self."

In addition to the structure and overall plan of Baldwin's first novel fitting so appropriately with its thematic emphasis, that structure also enables him to present his characters with their faults and strengths as full human beings, not as propagandistic embodiments of good and evil. Baldwin, in his essays on Harriet Beecher Stowe and Richard Wright, recognizes the dangers to artistic and realistic rendering of character that are presented by propaganda or protest fiction. In this novel he is dealing comprehensively and emotionally with the hot issue of race relations in the United States at a time, the early 1950s, when neither white ignorance and prejudice nor black powerlessness is conducive to holistic depictions of black experience. Nevertheless, by means of the flashbacks in Part II of *Go Tell It on the Mountain,* Baldwin leads us to understanding of and sympathy for his older characters, without minimizing their faults or magnifying their virtues.

One example here, too, will illustrate his technique. Gabriel, the closest thing the book has to a villain, can be understood and sympathized with, if not liked or admired or respected. Despite the havoc he wreaks in lives around him, he does not deliberately set out to harm anyone. He does ease his mother's dying. He defends Deborah against the jibes and jokes of other "holy" men. He marries her and does not make her as miserable as Florence later claims. Apart from his nine-day affair with Esther, he is apparently faithful to Deborah until her death. Most significantly, after marrying Elizabeth, adopting John, and having three further children of his own, he is still around. Gabriel's own father deserted his wife and children. Elizabeth's father defaulted. Richard deserted through suicide. Gabriel is the only adult male in the book who is still there, struggling to support and protect his family. Because we have his story through what he has gone through, the way he sees it, we can sympathize with and understand him even while we, with Johnnie, want to hate him.

Moving from the overall structure of *Go Tell It on the Mountain* to characteristics of its language, one is most dramatically struck by the Biblical allusions and religious imagery of the book. One not thoroughly familiar with the Bible, particularly the Old Testament, or with traditional hymns and prayers, particularly of American black churches, will miss many of the allusions. But when those allusions are discovered and examined, it is evident that the language Baldwin chooses supports his characters and themes throughout the novel.

The title of the book, from a Negro Spiritual, a Christmas song, is a first line of "Go tell it on the mountain, / Over the hills and everywhere; / Go tell it on the mountain, / That Jesus Christ is born." Earlier working titles of the book were "Crying Holy" and "In My Father's House." The birth declared in abbreviated fashion in the title finally chosen suggests the new birth of John, the step in his search for identity represented in his conversion at the end of the book.

Similarly, Biblical figures, including the Father and the Son, are used throughout *Go Tell It on the Mountain* as representing present-day human characters and relationships. In reaction to John's conversion, Gabriel bemoans the fact that "the son of the bondwoman stood where the rightful heir should stand." Gabriel thinks of himself as, and is seen by the reader as, Father Abraham, to whom a promise of fruitfulness was also given, and to whom Ishmael was born of the bondwoman, Hagar. The "rightful heir" was Isaac, born of Abraham's wife, Sarah, long after her period of fertility. Ishmael, the disinherited outcast, comes to us here in the form of John, figuratively if not literally disinherited, and suggests the disinherited, outcast black in American history. But Baldwin ironically twists some of his analogues, so here it is the stepson who stands to inherit Gabriel's preaching role, and the "rightful sons," Royal and Roy, who head for destruction. Just so, it may be that the outcast black in American history embodies our best legacy.

The guilt John Grimes is at least temporarily freed from by his conversion in Part III of *Go Tell It on the Mountain* is closely entwined with sex, with dirt, with skin color. The Old Testament metaphor including all these links is the story of Noah and his sons. In the deepest throes of John's preconversion threshing, as in his imagination his father seeks him out to beat him, John remembers his sin.

Yes, he had sinned: one morning, alone, in the dirty bathroom, in the square, dirt-gray cupboard room that was filled with the stink of his father. Sometimes, leaning over the cracked, "tattle-tale gray" bathtub, he scrubbed his father's back; and looked, as the accursed son of Noah had looked, on his father's hideous nakedness. It was secret, like sin, and slimy, like the serpent, and heavy, like the rod. Then he hated his father, and longed for the power to cut his father down. . . . Ah, that son of Noah's had been cursed down to the present groaning generation: *A servant of servants shall he be unto his brethren.*

Noah's and Ham's story is in Genesis 9:20–25. Despite its simplicity and brevity—a son looking on a drunken, naked father in his tent—the curse which Noah places on Ham and his descendants has long been taken historically to explain and justify enslavement of black people, supposed descendants of Ham. John confronts an engrained tradition connecting his dark skin with sin, and sex with sin.

It is no wonder, then, that release from guilt and sin gets tied up, as it does in the New Testament, with "washing whiter than snow." As Robert Bone points out, the church can be a "path of self-hatred" or a "path of self-acceptance," with Christ as a "kind of spiritual bleaching cream" or with the Negro challenging "the white man's moral categories." And Gabriel's example, unfortunately, follows the former, self-hating use of religion.[4]

There is in *Go Tell It on the Mountain,* however, a clear, if untested, representation of the church as a path to self-acceptance. In Elisha, John's new big-brother-in-the-Lord, John has a model of circumspect behavior, loving acts, boisterous joy. The "seal ineffaceable forever," Elisha's kiss on John's forehead at the conclusion of the book, becomes a kind of spiritual translation of the physical attraction suggested between the two young men. Elisha, Old Testament successor to the prophet Elijah, had even in death the ability to bring life. In 2 Kings 13 a dead man is flung into Elisha's tomb. No sooner has his body touched Elisha's bones than the dead man springs to life. In the novel, it is perhaps because of Elisha's young, untested innocence that his story appears only in the first and third parts, and that he can serve as such a positive, life-offering model. John has, it seems, at least three years of protection before him until he reaches the age of Elisha.

The end of *Go Tell It on the Mountain* is the beginning of a probable three-year truce for John Grimes with the sin and sex and danger of the avenue down which he returns home from the Tarry Service. The end of the novel is thus both optimistic and pessimistic, for the avenue, with its spittle, its spent sperm, its dirt, will still be there when John turns seventeen. A truce is not a peace treaty. John is, as it were, on spiritual parole from the imprisonment of his sexually-developing body, from the incarceration of his family conflicts, and from the entrapment of the ghetto.

Part of the basis for concluding what the novel does not explicitly nor implicitly state—that John can look forward to a three-year grace period—is of course the autobiographical core of the novel. Baldwin himself, converted at age fourteen, was a junior minister in a pentecostal church until age seventeen. Gabriel Grimes is clearly based on David Baldwin, and the long ten-year gestation of the novel is the time it took Baldwin to work out, mostly from Europe, the relationship his own youthful experiences, family history, racial history, and national history bore to his personal and artistic identity. Michel Fabre has suggested further that the father figure in *Go Tell It on the Mountain,* which the youthful Grimes must eschew, also represents Baldwin's working himself out of dependency on his erstwhile mentor, author Richard Wright.[5]

However much or little biographical Baldwin material is present in the reader's consideration of *Go Tell It on the Mountain,* it remains an extremely powerful, highly textured, repeatedly intriguing book. Passion and form, past and present, the universal and the particular, merge in the first of Baldwin's novels in ways not quite achieved again in his writing.

4

"Making love in the midst of mirrors": *Giovanni's Room* and *Another Country*

While *Go Tell It on the Mountain* was a means by which Baldwin could deal with his own youth, religious background, and family relationships, particularly with his father, his next two novels, *Giovanni's Room,* 1957, and *Another Country,* 1962, zero in more closely on another aspect of identity—sexuality. It might be even more accurate to say that, while *Go Tell It on the Mountain* uses religious experience as a prime metaphor for the search for identity, the next two novels use sexuality, particularly homosexuality, as the metaphor.

Giovanni's Room is the shorter, simpler, but somewhat more confusing and provisional of the two books. No Negro characters appear in *Giovanni's Room.* Settings are Paris and the south of France. Flashback is used here as it was in *Go Tell It on the Mountain,* but in a simplified way, with one character, David, a young white American, telling the entire story in first-person point of view.

The book is in two parts, with the first, shorter part, about 90 pages in the Dell paperback edition, made up of three chapters. The second part, 125 pages, consists of five chapters. The first part begins with David at the window of a "great house in the south of France" with night falling, looking at his increasingly distinct reflection in the glass. We learn immediately

that he will be leaving for Paris the following morning,
"the most terrible morning of my life"; that his "girl,"
Hella, is on her way back to America; that Giovanni is
"about to perish, sometime between this night and this
morning, on the guillotine." From this portentous information, we move in the rest of Chapter 1 back with
David to his early life up to his departure from America for France.

The events and personages of David's early life
include most significantly a homosexual experience
with a friend, Joe, an experience which David has
since lied about, even to himself. "I repent now—for
all the good it does—one particular lie among the many
lies I've told, told, lived, and believed." In addition,
his mother, dead when he was five,

figured in my nightmares, blind with worms, her hair as dry
as metal and brittle as a twig, straining to press me against
her body, that body so putrescent, so sickening soft, that it
opened, as a claw and cried, into a breach so enormous as
to swallow me alive.

His father and Aunt Ellen fight and argue about
the father's drunken affairs and David's own future, until he manages to escape from home in a job and in the
Army. "I had decided to allow no room in the universe
for something which shamed and frightened me. I
succeeded very well—by not looking at the universe,
by not looking at myself, by remaining, in effect, in
constant motion."

Weary of alcohol, "meaningless friendships,"
"desperate women," and work, he leaves for France, to
find himself. "If I had had any intimation that the self
I was going to find would turn out to be only the same
self from which I had spent so much time in flight,"
David now concludes, "I would have stayed home."
And yet, inevitable for his identity, he knows, "at the

very bottom of my heart," exactly what he is doing, as he sails off across the Atlantic.

Chapter 2 of *Giovanni's Room* gives a detailed description of David's meeting of Giovanni, a young Italian working in a Parisian bar frequented by gays. The setting and means of the meeting are important for contrast with the immediate, untainted, pure attraction and love Giovanni displays for David. David, out of money, is being fed by an American businessman, Jacques. Jacques and the Frenchman, Guillaume, who operates the bar, are repulsive, old homosexuals who spend their nights bribing and sampling the "knife-blade lean, tight-trousered boys" on the auction block. In contrast to the sordid buying and selling all around is Giovanni and his conversation with David, "so vivid, so winning, all of the light of that gloomy tunnel trapped around his head."

Chapter 3 of Part One takes us from the bar to a restaurant, for an early breakfast of oysters and wine, with, again, the purity of Giovanni's interest contrasted with the shopping around of Jacques and Guillaume. "And here my baby came indeed, through all that sunlight, his face flushed and his hair flying, his eyes, unbelievably, like morning stars." David and Giovanni end up in Giovanni's room—and "soon it was too late to do anything but moan" remembers David later. "He pulled me against him, putting himself into my arms as though he were giving me himself to carry, and slowly pulled me down with him to that bed. With everything in me screaming *No!* yet the sum of me sighed *Yes*."

Part One concludes back in the great house in the south of France, with unseasonal snow falling and with the landlady coming to inventory her property. David imagines her to be Giovanni's mother. "It is terrible how naked she makes me feel, like a half-grown boy, naked before his mother." After she leaves, David

again remembers Giovanni, comparing his imminent
death with their life together.

I suppose they will come for him early in the morning, perhaps just before dawn, so that the last thing Giovanni will
ever see will be that grey, lightless sky over Paris, beneath
which we stumbled homeward together so many desperate
and drunken mornings.

Part One of *Giovanni's Room* records David's
growing acceptance of his sexuality, his acceptance of
Giovanni's love. Part Two records his subsequent fall
from acceptance, his denial of himself, his feeling, his
possibility.

Much of the denial is expressed in terms of the
growing repugnance David has for Giovanni's room,
in which they now both live. "I remember that life in
that room seemed to be occurring beneath the sea"
begins Chapter 1 of Part Two. Soon negative imagery
takes over in the descriptions of the room, just as
springtime in their first coming together is overtaken by
summer and then winter, as Giovanni kills Guillaume
and hides, then is captured, tried, and executed. David
fears the desire that Giovanni's love has awakened in
him for other boys, and the images of Jacques's and
Guillaume's perpetual and sordid seeking that the desire condemns him to.

The beast which Giovanni had awakened in me would never
go to sleep again; but one day I would not be with Giovanni
any more. And would I then, like all the others, find myself
turning and following all kinds of boys down God knows
what dark avenues, into what dark places?

With this fearful intimation there opened in me a hatred
for Giovanni which was as powerful as my love and which
was nourished by the same roots.

Chapter 2 brings us back to David's growing
feeling of entrapment in Giovanni's room. "It became,

in a way, every room I had ever been in and every room I find myself in hereafter. . . . Life in that room seemed to be occurring underwater, as I say, and it is certain that I underwent a sea change there." The room is now closely described—its smallness, its curtainless and white-painted windows, its torn wallpaper on the floor together with dirty laundry, suitcases, tools, paint-brushes. It is not, as Giovanni calls it, the garbage heap of Paris but, as David now sees it, "Giovanni's regur-gitated life." The room is tied with David's potential for saving Giovanni with his love: "I was to destroy this room and give Giovanni a new and better life. This life could only be my own, which in order to transform Giovanni's, must first become a part of Giovanni's room."

David's retreat from Giovanni and his room is aided by a letter from his girl, Hella, who had gone off to Spain to consider marriage to him. "I've decided to let two try it," she finally writes. "This business of lov-ing me, I mean." To reassure himself that he is still capable of making love to a woman, he picks up and briefly uses a chubby American girl, Sue.

Chapter 3 narrates the best and worst of Gio-vanni's and David's life together. Giovanni loses his job because he will not submit to Guillaume's sex acts and despairingly clings to David. David feels "that Judas and the Savior had met in me." The intrusion of the present in his memory-flashback sees the hours of the night dwindle. "I know," says David, "that no mat-ter what I do, anguish is about to overtake me in this house, as naked and silver as that great knife which Giovanni will be facing very soon." Giovanni's im-prisonment in his body and in his prison cell are no dif-ferent, it seems, than David's imprisonment in his body and his renounced responsibility. His reflections accuse him: "My executioners are here with me, walking up and down with me, washing things and packing and drinking from my bottle. . . . walls, windows, mirrors, water, the night outside—they are everywhere."

Chapters 4 and 5 tell the story of Hella's return to Paris, David's desertion of Giovanni, Giovanni's turning to Jacques and then other men for support, and his ultimate strangling of Guillaume in despair and rage after submitting to him in order to recover his barkeeping job. When David returns to Giovanni's room to pick up his things, we learn of Giovanni's past in the little Italian village, of the death of his young child, which caused him to leave. "And you will have no idea of the life there," he tells David, "dripping and bursting and beautiful and terrible, as you have no idea of my life now." "You want to be *clean,*" he accuses David. "You think you came here covered with soap and you think you will go out covered with soap—and you do not want to *stink,* not even for five minutes, in the meantime." David realizes that in "fleeing from his body, I confirmed and perpetuated his body's power over me."

Giovanni hides from the police for a week after the murder, but is ultimately found and in short order tried and convicted and sentenced. David tries fleeing with Hella to the south, where it should be, but isn't, warmer. He takes violent refuge in her body until it becomes "stale," "uninteresting," her presence "grating." Ultimately, Hella discovers him in a bar with a sailor and knows the truth of his relationship to Giovanni. She leaves for America.

Giovanni's Room concludes in the early morning in the "great house in the south of France," with David imagining Giovanni's advance to his execution as his own reflection in the large window panes becomes more and more faint. "I seem to be fading away before my eyes." He forces himself to look at his body in the mirror. "It is trapped in my mirror as it is trapped in time and it hurries toward revelation. . . . I long to crack that mirror and be free. . . . The key to my salvation, which cannot save my body, is hidden in my flesh."

David leaves the house, locks it, with the morning weighing "on my shoulders with the dreadful weight of hope." He tears up the blue envelope in which came the news of Giovanni's death sentence and throws the pieces into the wind. "Yet as I turn and begin walking toward the waiting people, the wind blows some of them back on me." So ends *Giovanni's Room*.

Some critics have described *Giovanni's Room* as a kind of first draft or trial run for *Another Country*, particularly in its use of sexuality, and especially male homosexuality, as a metaphor for the search for identity, for an understanding of life and responsibility to others within it, for the possibilities of rebirth.

The problem with *Giovanni's Room*, its provisional quality, lies in the personage of David. He cannot, and does not, as a character carry the weight of meaning Baldwin is apparently trying to place on his experience. Because he rejects the possibilities his relationship with Giovanni contains, he becomes a negative, and confusing, embodiment of homosexual experience, particularly for a reader already having negative images of that experience. The reader can't help but feel that David has perhaps made the right decision, even while he or she knows that, to Baldwin, the decision is cowardly.

Giovanni's statements to David about his wanting to get through life in soapy cleanliness, without "stink," and the selection of a white American for the main character of *Giovanni's Room* are of course related. Baldwin in his essays continually castigates the white American male for his refusal to admit or see or understand the "darker side" of life. And fear of "the terror within" has inevitably led to the easier and "safer" creating of external "evils" [2]—black men, homosex-

uals. Upright, defiantly heterosexual David, in his will-
ful innocence of "the stink of life," is in explicit contrast with bisexual, southern European Giovanni and,
in implied contrast, with the black American whose experiences early on force him into realistic confrontation
of the "terror within."

The hope for David's rebirth into understanding
is in Giovanni's room, womblike in its close, cluttered
darkness, its watery imagery. But David, in this experience at least, refuses to be born the hard, messy
way, so of course cannot be born at all. The slight suggestion of hope at the end of the novel, with the small
bits of the blue envelope of the death sentence carried back onto David by the wind, means, perhaps, that
he will have another chance to do what he has failed
to do this time around—be reborn through terror and
loss of innocence. He cannot love at all, the book tells
us through Hella, until he undergoes that torturous rebirth. In a 1963 interview, Baldwin stated very clearly
that because American men are afraid of homosexuality, "they don't know how to go to bed with women
either." ("Disturber of the Peace," by E. Auchincloss
and N. Lynch, *Mademoiselle,* May 1963, p. 206.)

The difficulty with *Giovanni's Room* is in its simplicity. The story of Giovanni is more melodramatic
than realistic. It must be melodramatic, probably, to
hold a reader's attention for the point of the book.
The point of the book, too, while interesting, seems too
simple. Even a reader cheerfully admitting the importance of sexuality in all forms is likely to find the
weight of human identity carried by a homosexual affair not just simple, but simplistic.

Baldwin does not make the mistake of oversim-
plifying again. In *Another Country,* while the same
meaning and potential are given to the homosexual
experience, meaning and potential for identity do not

lie only there, but in several ways of seeing the "darker side" of life—heterosexual experience, interracial experience, music and writing and death.

And the plot and characterizations of *Another Country* are nothing if not complex. The novel is divided into three books: "Easy Rider," "Any Day Now," and "Toward Bethlehem," with the third, the book of resolutions, much shorter than the other two. The characters and characters' relationships are carefully representative of black and white; male and female; married and unmarried; homosexual, bisexual, and heterosexual. Resolutions are also carefully spread between failure and death, love and happiness, and continuing struggle with no clear positive or negative outcome yet in sight.

The long first chapter of the first book belongs to a black jazz drummer, Rufus Scott. His story begins at Times Square, New York City, past midnight, in the late fall. He has been sitting in movies since 2:00; he has not eaten for days; he is broke. In characteristic Baldwin style, here in third-person point of view, we move back and forth in the chapter between this present tense—Rufus Scott at the end of his rope—and his mind's going back over the events of his life that have brought him there. His theme, the song line "You took the best, so why not take the rest?" occurs early, in connection with the "caterpillar fingers between his thighs" that he must fight off in the movie theater. He is "one of the fallen," under the "weight" of the "murderous" city, alone, "part of an unprecedented multitude."

Taking his memories not in the order in which they weave through his mind, but in chronological order, we find Rufus as an introduction to, a kind of negative touchstone for, the characters who make up the rest of the novel. Rufus grew up in Harlem, admired, talented, believed in, the idol of his younger sister,

Ida, and hope of his parents. But the image in his memory is of a drowned boy being carried by his father from the garbage-filled Hudson River. And his memory of Army bootcamp in the South is "the shoe of a white officer against his mouth," which is on the ground, "against the red, dusty clay."

Back in New York, Rufus achieves some fame in hip circles as a drummer. He becomes friends with Vivaldo Moore, a struggling writer of Brooklyn Italian background; Cass and Richard Silenski, she an ex-New England debutante, he a Polish immigrant's son, English teacher, and writer; and Eric Jones, a red-headed actor from a well-to-do Alabama family. It is with Eric that Rufus's love-hate needs are acted out most violently and cruelly, in a triple reaction to Eric's whiteness, Southernness, and homosexuality. Later Rufus vents the same frustrated, tortured destructive drive on Leona, a poor Southern white woman who has been forced to leave her child behind in the South. Rufus's enactment of love and hate, tenderness and beatings, on the body of Leona leads eventually to her institutionalization and his degeneration to the state in which we find him at the opening of the novel. It is largely the hostile intrusion of "the big world" on Rufus that destroys his love relationships—"trouble with the landlord, with the neighbors, with all the adolescents in the Village," with his family, with the ever-menacing police. Rufus resents them all.

In total despair now—no job, money, home—Rufus finds the only friend he has left, Vivaldo, and eats and drinks with him, Cass, and Richard in a bar backroom. When Cass and Richard leave and Vivaldo is joined by an old girlfriend, Jane, Rufus wanders out to go to the bathroom, but instead heads uptown and eventually to the George Washington bridge. He jumps, as did Baldwin's young friend on whom Rufus Scott is based.

He was black and the water was black. . . .

The wind tore at him, at his head and shoulders, while something in him screamed, why? why? He thought of Eric. . . . *I can't make it this way.* He thought of Ida. He whispered, I'm sorry, Leona, and then the wind took him, he felt himself going over, head down, the wind, the stars, the lights, the water, all rolled together, *all right. . . . All right, you motherfucking Godalmighty bastard. I'm coming to you.*

Chapter 2 brings us closer to understanding the world and the characters of Cass and Richard and Vivaldo. The chapter opens the following Sunday morning, amid Sunday papers and coffee cups in the Silenski's living room in a Puerto Rican neighborhood in West Side Manhattan. Ida Scott calls and comes over, worried about her brother, and Vivaldo comes to read the novel Richard has just sold. The Silenski's marriage looks idyllic—two sons, Richard on the verge of success and fame. Vivaldo is interested, from a distance, in Ida.

By Wednesday, the day before Thanksgiving, Rufus's body has been found. In Richard's and Cass's reactions to the suicide, we begin to see a crack, an uncertainty in the idyllic marriage, a menace to safety. At Rufus's funeral, Vivaldo and Cass are the only whites, and again, for Cass, there is a suggestion of danger, of depth, of worlds she is not familiar with or comfortable with. Simultaneously, she recognizes in Richard's book the extent of his talent and courage—"It had been written because he was afraid, afraid of things dark, strange, dangerous, difficult, and deep."

Rufus's funeral takes Vivaldo back to his own origins. " 'You had to be a man where I come from, and you had to prove it, prove it all the time. . . . Well, my Dad's still there, sort of helping to keep the liquor industry going. Most of the kids I knew are dead or in jail or on junk.' " One of his boyhood proofs of manhood was beating up a "queer" from Greenwich

Village. " 'There were seven of us, and we made him go down on all of us and we beat the piss out of him and took all his money and took his clothes and left him lying on the cement floor, and, you know, it was winter.' "

Cass realizes that "Vivaldo's recollections in no sense freed him from the things he recalled." She mentally articulates a key to Rufus's failure and the struggles of the other characters:

Perhaps such secrets, the secrets of everyone, were only expressed when the person laboriously dragged them into the light of the world, imposed them on the world, and made them a part of the world's experience. Without this effort, the secret place was merely a dungeon in which the person perished; without this effort, indeed, the entire world would be an uninhabitable darkness.

Chapter 3 of "Easy Rider" opens several months later, in March of the following year. Vivaldo is struggling with characters of his novel who will not "surrender up to him their privacy"; "they were waiting for him to find the key, press the nerve, tell the truth." He realizes their similarity to himself and wonders "whether or not he had ever, really, been present at his life" or whether he, like others, had passed his life "in a kind of limbo of denied and unexamined pain." He reviews his relationship to women, to men, to blacks, and recalls his first meeting of Ida and his only meeting of Ida's and Rufus's mother.

Ida, whom Vivaldo is taking to lunch and a literary party at the Silenskis', reviews a different kind of life. "She was always waiting for the veiled insult or the lewd suggestion. And she had good reason for it, she was not being fantastical or perverse. It was the way the world treated girls with bad reputations and every colored girl had been born with one."

The Silenskis are "climbing that well-known ladder," with increasing unhappiness. They have moved to a "gray, anonymous building" with "functionless pillars" and "an immense plain of imitation marble and leather." " 'He's not even famous *yet,'* " says Cass, " 'and, already I can't stand it. Somehow, it just seems to reduce itself to having drinks and dinners with lots of people you certainly wouldn't be talking to if they weren't . . . in the profession.' " Cass points out to Vivaldo and Ida that their acting friend, Eric Jones, is coming back from France to star in a Broadway production.

All goes well with Ida and Vivaldo this day. Their enjoyment of each other is broken only, and briefly, by Vivaldo's jealousy of Ida's attention to a TV producer, Mr. Ellis. They leave the Silenskis' party, however, go to Vivaldo's apartment, and make love for the first time. This chapter and Book One end appropriately on a Spring afternoon, with Ida making coffee and singing: "If you can't give me a dollar, / Give me a lousy dime— / Just want to feed / This hungry man of mine."

Book Two, "Any Day Now," opens in a kind of Eden, not in New York City. "Eric sat naked in his rented garden. Flies buzzed and boomed in the brilliant heat, and a yellow bee circled his head. . . . Yves' tiny black-and-white kitten stalked the garden as though it were Africa. . . . The house and garden overlooked the sea." Down below, in the Mediterranean, Eric's lover, Yves, is swimming. It is the day before their leaving this house to return to Paris, from whence Eric will go to New York, to be joined there later by Yves. The first chapter of this central book gives the reader a full history of Yves, of Eric's youth and early homosexual experiences in Alabama, and of their meeting and their growing love.

Significantly, Yves and Eric first become lovers after three months of seeing one another every day, in the town of Chartres, under the shadow of the great

cathedral towers. Eric during these months "purified,
as well as he could, his house, and opened his doors;
established a precarious order in the heart of chaos,"
removing that "army of lonely men who had used
him . . . [as] the receptacle of an anguish which he
could scarcely believe was in the world." He has
thereby won Yves's trust, for Yves has also been used.

In a room above a stream, their first moment
physically together "obliterated, cast into the sea of
forgetfulness, all the sordid beds and squalid grap-
pling which had led [them] here." "Eric felt beneath his fingers Yves's slowly stirring, stiffening sex.
This sex dominated the long landscape of his life as
the cathedral towers dominated the plains."

The key to Eric's importance in the novel lies in
his exclusion from the standards of the world and the
subsequent need for him to develop his own code of
honor.

He knew that he had no honor which the world could recognize. His life, passions, trials, loves, were, at worst, filth,
and, at best, disease in the eyes of the world, and crimes in
the eyes of his countrymen. . . . There were no standards
for him because he could not accept the definitions, the
hideously mechanical jargon of the age. There was no one
around him worth his envy, he did not believe in the vast,
gray sleep which was called security, did not believe in the
cures, panaceas, and slogans which afflicted the world he
knew; and this meant that he had to create his standards
and make up his definitions as he went along.

Yves and Eric make love the last night above the
sea—Yves "called Eric's name as no one had ever called
this name before. Eric, Eric. Eric. The sound of his
breath filled Eric, heavier than the far-off pounding
of the sea." Chapter 1 of this second and central book
of the novel ends in the peaceful, sunny morning with
the two about "to make tracks."

The second chapter of the book sees Eric in New York eight days later. "Why am I going home? he asked himself. But he knew why. It was time. In order not to lose all that he had gained, he had to move forward and risk it all." The menace of New York is intensified for Eric after his French experience—its "note of . . . buried despair," its "blighted" boys, its raging "plague," its people "at home with, accustomed to, brutality and indifference, and . . . terrified of human affection."

Shortly, he sees the menace in the lives of his friends. He visits Cass and Richard. Their sons are beaten up in Central Park by black kids and the Silenskis fight in front of Eric. Richard releases his long resentment of Cass's reaction to his "success," and exhibits castration fear.

"You're just like all the other American cunts. You want a guy you can feel sorry for, you love him as long as he's helpless. Then you can *pitch in* . . . , you can be his *helper*. *Helper!* . . . Then, one fine day, the guy feels chilly between his legs and feels around for his cock and balls and finds she's helped herself to them and locked them in the linen closet."

Eric goes to the bar where Ida has her singing debut. She is a success. " 'My God,' " mutters Vivaldo, " 'she's been working,' " implying "that he had not been, and held an unconscious resentment." As Ellis appears, there is, Eric senses, "something very ugly in the air." Ida has been in contact with Ellis without Vivaldo's knowledge. As the four walk to another bar for a drink and a "business deal" between Ida and Ellis, Eric is menaced also by the policemen encountered, by the gay men they meet, by everything in the New York surroundings.

The following chapter, Chapter 3, develops these

suggested complications further. Cass talks to Vivaldo
about her marriage, goes off to sit in a movie alone,
and then calls Eric and goes to his apartment. To
Vivaldo's offer of company, she replies " 'No, Vivaldo,
thank you. I don't want to be protected any more.' "
As she and Eric venture into an affair with no future,
Eric says " 'Something is happening between us which
I don't really understand, but I'm willing to trust it. I
have the feeling, somehow, that I *must* trust it!' " Eric
introduces Cass to an unsafe, treacherous, but real "vision of the world" through his past experiences.

Meanwhile, Vivaldo is struggling with his doubts
about, his battles with, Ida. The trust he feels com-
pelled to have is based, however, not on admission of
what he knows, but on blindness to it. She is not
home; she is not at work; she is undoubtedly with
Ellis. Vivaldo wanders through bars and ends up,
eventually, at an all-night pot party, which seems to
serve little function in the novel except to give Baldwin
a chance to describe it before it becomes an American
commonplace.

Vivaldo's soul-searching contains echoes of Gabriel's Bible passage in *Go Tell It on the Mountain*
and of Eric's three-month preparation for Yves's love.
"What order could prevail against so grim a privacy?
And yet without order, of what value was the mystery?
Order. Order. *Set thine house in order.*" He recognizes
where he must go, in order to "break through" with
Ida, with suggestions of Eric's and Yves's experience
and of the surrender that David in *Giovanni's Room*
refuses to make. "And something in him was break-
ing; he was, briefly and horribly, in a region where
there were no definitions of any kind neither of color,
nor of male and female. There was only the leap and
the rending and the terror and the surrender." He confronts the chainlinks between sex and sin and color
jangling through *Go Tell It on the Mountain*.

How did he take her, what did he bring to her? . . . If he despised his flesh, then he must despise hers—and *did* he despise his flesh? And if she despised her flesh, then she must despise him. . . . What were all those fucking confessions about? *I have sinned in thought and deed.*

Chapter 4 of "Any Day Now" takes the complications to climax. Ida's and Vivaldo's conflicts are exaggerated by the New York summer heat—"there was [sic] speedily accumulating . . . great areas of the unspoken, vast minefields which neither dared to cross." " 'How can you love somebody you don't know anything about? You don't know where I've been. You don't know what life is like for me. . . . Nobody's willing to pay their dues,' " Ida accuses.

Cass's and Eric's affair continues, and Eric's theatrical success mounts—a movie role, a screen test for the lead in Dostoyevski's *The Possessed.* Eric's acting power is tied to his, by this time, clearly androgynous sexuality—"There was great force in [his] face, and great gentleness. But, as most women are not gentle, nor most men strong, it was a face which suggested, resonantly, in the depths, the truth about our natures."

On the climactic night, Vivaldo and Eric go off to Eric's apartment for searching conversation, and Ida and Cass, supposedly going home, are taken by Ida instead to Harlem to meet Ellis. Ida's most negative view of events is voiced in her warning to Cass.

"What you people don't know . . . is that life is a *bitch,* baby. It's the biggest hype going. You don't have any experience in paying your dues and it's going to be rough on you, baby, when the deal goes down. There's lots of back dues to be collected, and I know damn well you haven't got a penny saved."

And, indeed, Cass's promissory notes start coming in that night, as she comes home to face Richard's accusations and beating.

When she had been safe and respectable, so had the world been safe and respectable; now the entire world was bitter with deceit and danger and loss; and which was the greater illusion? . . . Richard had been her protection, not only against the evil in the world, but also against the wilderness of herself. And now she would never be protected again. She tried to feel jubilant about this. But she did not feel jubilant. She felt frightened and bewildered.

The final book of the novel is called "Toward Bethlehem" and has a Shakespearean epigraph from Sonnet LXV: "How with this rage shall beauty hold a plea, / Whose action is no stronger than a flower?" The beauty of the first chapter of the final book is placed in a total physical and spiritual love experience between Eric and Vivaldo. "It was [Vivaldo's] first sexual encounter with a male in many years, and his very first sexual encounter with a friend." He is involved in a "blacker and more pure" mystery than ever before.

He held Eric very tightly and covered Eric's body with his own, as though he were shielding him from the falling heavens. But it was also as though he were, at the same instant, being shielded—by Eric's love. It was strangely and insistently double-edged, it was like making love in the midst of mirrors, or it was like death by drowning. . . . Vivaldo seemed to have fallen through a great hole in time, back to his innocence; he felt clear, washed, and empty, waiting to be filled.

This beauty, surrender, and acceptance enable Vivaldo to go back to Ida, to listen to her confession, know her, trust her in a new way. Vivaldo is also now able to write, and Ida is relieved of her entirely isolated, negative view of the world—someone has heard.

Cass is left in the midst of struggle, with no clear outcome. She meets Eric, explains Richard's anger, wonders what she will do, fears losing her children. " 'You did something very valuable for me, Eric,' " she tells him. " 'You've been my love and now you're my friend. . . . That was you you gave me for a little while. It was really you.' "

The ultimate beauty is reserved for the final three-page chapter of *Another Country*. Yves flies in to New York from Paris. Eric is there to meet him: "all [Yves's] fear left him, he was certain, now, that everything would be all right. . . . Then even his luggage belonged to him again, and he strode through the barriers, more high-hearted than he had ever been as a child, into that city which the people from heaven had made their home." So ends *Another Country*.

Since the central characters in *Another Country* are clearly Rufus Scott and Eric Jones, it is useful to explore their similarities and differences as Baldwin depicts them. Rufus dominates the first part of the book as Eric dominates the last part, with Rufus's memories introducing us to Eric and Eric's memories enabling us to understand more of Rufus. Rufus is black, Northern, urban. Eric is white, Southern, small town. Rufus is a talented, personable musician; Eric is an actor. Rufus's life ends in suicide; Eric's is headed for love and success. Knowing these superficial facts, one might assume Rufus's failure to be a function of his race, Eric's success a function of his. Not so, or not entirely so.

Baldwin seems to suggest with these two characters that while pain and suffering are inevitable, acceptance of pain, necessary for being a fully aware, alive human, is not. And love, translated into *hearing* another person's pain, while necessary for accepting that pain, is hard to come by. The world gets in the way a lot. United States racism gets in the way a lot. New York streets, New York policemen get in the way a lot.

The key difference between Rufus's failure and Eric's success seems to lie in that otherworldly, other-country experience that Eric achieves only by leaving the United States and living in France. Yves is free of the racial and sexual hang-ups peculiar to American

men. The love experience with Yves, blessed as it is
by purification and cathedral-shadowing, enables Eric
to come back to New York and bring with him some of
that androgynous love that he gives Cass and Vivaldo. He must be out of the country, it seems, to
formulate that code of honor of his own.

Eric's suffering because of his homosexuality is
made excruciatingly clear in *Another Country*. But the
shame and misery and fear he undergoes are his means
to heroism because he does come out on the other side.
His flesh is redeemed. He is heard and seen as his
acting is empowered by his suffering. Rufus, on the
other hand, suffers shame and fear and misery and is
not heard, is not understood. His drumming art is in a
code more difficult to translate than is Eric's. And
Rufus's New York audience is less free or less willing
to make the translation. Vivaldo makes the translation,
through Ida, only after Rufus's death. Cass comes close
to making it the night of Rufus's suicide. Ida does not
need to translate, for Ida uses the same musical code.
But Ida is not there during Rufus's last month.
Richard's character is confirmed as weak and inad-
mirable by his willingness to condemn Rufus for his
treatment of Leona. Richard is farthest from understanding.

Eric does understand, when he learns while
abroad what has become of Rufus. Fittingly, it is the
suffering that Rufus has put Eric through that is part
of what enables Eric to bring blessing to Vivaldo and
through Vivaldo to Ida. On the evening of their conversation and love, Vivaldo asks Eric about his relationship to Rufus, comparing it to his and Ida's. " 'She
never lets me forget I'm white, she never lets me forget
she's colored. And I don't care, I don't care—did
Rufus do that to you? Did he try to make you pay?' "
" 'Ah,' " Eric replies. " 'He didn't *try*. I paid. . . . But
I'm not sad about it any more. If it hadn't been for

Rufus, I would never have had to go away, I would never have been able to deal with Yves.' "

It is also in Eric's and Vivaldo's post-lovemaking conversation that what could be called "the moral of the story" is articulated. " 'I think that you can begin to *become* admirable if, when you're hurt, you don't try to pay back. . . . Perhaps if you can accept the pain that almost kills you, you can use it, you can become better,' " says Vivaldo. Eric agrees and adds, " 'Otherwise, you just get stopped with whatever it was that ruined you and you make it happen over and over again and your life has—ceased, really—because you can't move or change or love any more.' "

The point, the moral, the lesson is not so new; but Baldwin's way of conveying it in *Another Country* has some positive and unique qualities. Making sex and racial conflict both explicit and significant; using the New York setting so thoroughly and skillfully; making music such an integral part of character and thought; using language with honesty and power—these are some of the ways Baldwin gives the novel and the moral his distinctive fictional stamp.

Honesty in language may bother some readers. But the bluntness of the language is part of Baldwin's message about facing up to reality. At one point in *Giovanni's Room,* David bemoans to Giovanni the fact that " 'people have very dirty words for—for this situation.' " Giovanni replies in words we can take as Baldwin's explanation for his using language as he does: " 'If dirty words frighten you, . . . I really do not know how you have managed to live so long. People are full of dirty words. The only time they do not use them, most people I mean, is when they are describing something dirty.' "

If the ending of *Another Country* is a bit dangling and unconvincing, the attempts to convey "normal" American life a bit bland, the overall structure not realizably organic, and the sentiment of the sex scenes sometimes exaggerated, it is nevertheless a highly read-able and memorable book. And the positive point it makes about love and hope, given the torturous means of attaining them, is positive indeed.

5

"You can say I'm the girl, or the boy, or their unborn child": *Tell Me How Long the Train's Been Gone* and *If Beale Street Could Talk*

"The heart attack was strange—fear is strange." With this opening line, thirty-nine-year-old Leo Proudhammer begins his first-person narration of *Tell Me How Long the Train's Been Gone*. The serious heart attack, on stage in San Francisco, of this fictitious black actor provides the basis in the novel for typical Baldwin reminiscing into the past of the character and inspires, briefly, at the end of the novel a possible major turning point in belief and action for that same character.

In the flashbacks to Leo Proudhammer's earlier life, we find typical Baldwin themes as well: the menacing city, particularly the Harlem ghetto; the false or temporary escape from menace provided by religion; art as communication of pain; the alienation of the Black artist from both white friends and black family; the spiritual significance of love experience; interracial love as both tormenting and liberating.

In the third and final section of the novel, "Black Christopher," we find a somewhat ambiguous change in political and social philosophy suggested for

Leo Proudhammer and, by implication, for James Baldwin. Whether the militance in Proudhammer's response
to words of black nationalist Christopher, "We need
us some guns," is carefully considered and deeply felt
or a desperate reaction to the pressures of the time (the
novel was published in 1968), it, nevertheless, suggests
a solution that Baldwin has not offered previously in
his novels.

The novel consists of three books without chapter divisions, each making up about one-third of the
whole. Book One is called "The House Nigger" and is
prefaced by a quotation from poet W. H. Auden: "In
the prison of his days, / Teach the free man how to
praise." The intent of the title of Book One is evidently
to suggest that Leo Proudhammer's early experiences
in the ghetto and as a novice actor lead him to a kind
of semi-privileged position in American society as a
"house slave" rather than a "field slave."

The sensations of Proudhammer's heart attack are
closely described, partly in terms of natural images:
an icy void; breathing louder than a cataract; scratchy,
loud, "sandstorm" breathing; an "unanswerable tide"
betraying a swimmer; panic "distant like the wind."
Barbara King, a central character, is introduced as she
holds onto the sick Leo. "We had known each other
for many years; starved together, worked together,
loved each other, suffered each other, made love;
and yet the most tremendous consummation of our
love was occurring now, as she patiently, in love and
terror, held my hand."

The love in "just holding on" sheds light for the
ill Proudhammer on the "desperately treacherous lab-
yrinth" of his life. The first memory which comes to
him is of his elder brother, Caleb, being taken away to
prison. We feel a sense of loss with his memories of
Caleb, and we are also set to wonder what has become

of him, for even Proudhammer's recalling the African belief that in death one returns to one's ancestors causes him to think: *"But I won't see Caleb."*

Remembering Caleb leads to remembering his parents, his proud but helpless father from Barbados, his light-colored mother from New Orleans. His parents are evoked in ghetto survival activities—holding off the tenant landlord, getting food on an already overextended grocery account. In the rhythm of the family's life, Caleb's Saturday evening task of taking little Leo to the movies leads to some of Leo's first adventures and terrors outside the ghetto. For Caleb, who is seven years older, usually goes off with his friends, leaving Leo to fend for himself. "Underground," on the subways, he recalls, "I received my first apprehension of New York neighborhoods, and, underground, first felt what may be called civic terror. I very soon realized that after the train had passed a certain point, going uptown or downtown, all the colored people disappeared."

Much of the danger Leo encounters or avoids, from getting beaten up by kids his own age to being harassed by policemen, is expressed in terms of terror of people's eyes. "I could no longer bear his eyes or anybody's eyes," he says of the ticket-taker at a movie theater. "I memorized the eyes, the contemptuous eyes," he says of two white policemen who stop and frisk Leo and Caleb. "I wished I were God. And then I hated God."

We are taken forward again to the time of the heart attack, to Proudhammer's removal to the white-walled hospital, to the demands of his "troubling, tyrannical, inconvenient flesh," and then again we are drawn back. This time we are taken back to his first struggling days in Greenwich Village with Barbara, fresh from her wealthy Kentucky home, and other poor but sensitive artist-types. "We called this place Paradise Alley—odd it is, to reflect now that in some way we loved it."

Much of this recall episode is spent on a theatrical party, which Barbara and Leo essentially crash, and which gives them their introduction to Saul and Lola San Marquand, who hire them for their first summer stock theater work. "It may have been that night that I really decided to attempt to become an actor. . . . It is certain that this night brought into my mind, in an astounding way, the great question of where the boundaries of reality were truly to be found." It is on this night that Proudhammer recognizes "the possibility of creating my language out of my pain, of using my pain to create myself. . . . My pain was the horse that I must learn to ride."

Barbara's visit to the hospital introduces the memory of Black Christopher, agent of our "journey through hell," in her words. We go back then in Proudhammer's thoughts, not to an explanation of that hellish journey, but to another event, a rally at which Proudhammer speaks and is protected from the crowd by Christopher. As a young black girl sings, "Deliverance will come. . . . I know it will come," Proudhammer thinks, "Christopher did not believe that deliverance would ever come—he was going to drag it down from heaven or raise it up from hell." About this new militance, he wonders, "Was Christopher's manner of deliverance worth the voices it would silence? Or would new songs come?"

Another return to the hospital in Proudhammer's consciousness, and the drifting once more into the past, take us to an elaboration of the first memory of this first book, Caleb's arrest and removal to prison. The extreme pain of the remembered event is now fully explored. About theater, Proudhammer has said:

There is a truth in the theater and there is a truth in life—they meet, but they are not the same, for life, God help us, *is* the truth. And those disguises which an artist wears are his means, not of fleeing from the truth, but of attempting to approach it.

It is as though, structurally, Proudhammer has had to approach the full truth of his life obliquely through his remembering related events, before facing, in memory, the events causing deepest pain.

The first Book, "House Nigger," ends with little Leo running screaming after the squad car that drives his beloved brother out of one ghetto and into a worse one. Leo cannot be comforted. "My father tried to stroke my head. I pushed his hand away. My mother offered me a bowl of soup. I knocked the bowl from her hand. I hate you, I said, I hate you, and I buried myself in the pillow which still held Caleb's smell."

The title of Book Two is "Is There Anybody There? said the traveler," and the epigraph is from musician Fats Waller, "Ain't misbehaving. / Saving myself for you." This portion of the novel approaches Proudhammer's painful memory in a slightly different way than did Book One, but also obliquely. The entire Book Two takes place in flashback; the hospital does not intrude. The primary flashback is to the summer stock theater experience, and the beginning of Proudhammer and Barbara's long but disjointed affair. Within *that* flashback we go back further, to Caleb's return from prison and subsequent departure from home. The most painful memory of the central book is, in other words, imbedded in the other memory of Proudhammer's first theater exposure.

The Actors' Means Workshop, run by Lola and Saul San Marquand, is located in a small New England town, which does not approve of the young, black Leo living with the white "kids" who paint signs, fetch food, sort costumes, mow lawns, pose nude for "Life classes" enrolled in by white matrons. Community hostility is understood rather than expressed, as long as three characters are seen together—Leo, Barbara, and Jerry, a huge, gentle white man of Italian descent. But on the three days that are the center of Proudhammer's memory of the workshop, all that changes.

Leo, Barbara, and Jerry pool their coins one Saturday night to eat at a local pizza restaurant, and are joined first by Madeleine, a blond leading player in a summer production, and then by two black working men, one local, from the other side of town, one traveling through. The latter, the younger of the two, reminds Leo of Caleb. The all-night party of the group, eating, drinking, dancing, talking, first in the white part of town, then, later, in the black, ends with Leo going home with Madeleine.

Trouble comes late the next day, when Leo is seen leaving her apartment by a terrified elderly couple and is subsequently hunted out, picked up, and jailed without charges, by the police. It is after his release, engineered by the Marquands, that Barbara tells Jerry, and then Leo, that it is really Leo she loves. She is wise to the ugly realities to be faced by an interracial couple, married or unmarried. " 'It's lucky I'm an actress. I mean—nothing comes before that. . . . And that helps me somehow. . . . We must be great. That's all we'll have. That's the only way we won't lose each other,' " she predicts, accurately, as it turns out. About Leo's bisexuality, she says, " 'Why should it bother me, Leo? I'm not in your body, I can't live your life. I only want to *share* your life.' "

Book Two ends with the aftermath of Barbara and Leo's first theatrical tryout with Saul that same day. The interracial love scene they do from Clifford Odets's *Waiting for Lefty* is now passionately informed by their newly admitted love. But to Saul, who cannot himself accept their love, their execution is too influenced by their personal relationship. " 'One's motives may always be personal. But one's execution . . . can never be personal,' " he tells Barbara. And for Leo he saves his most carefully disguised defeatism. " 'There is nothing wrong with aiming too high. Frankly, we think it possible that you *must* aim too high. We are not here to discourage. But we must tell you when we feel that you are aiming at a target which it will simply be impossible for you ever to reach.' "

" 'Fuck 'em.' " " 'They can go fuck themselves,' " is Leo's response as he leaves Jerry, asking his forgiveness, and then taking off in the Workshop car for New York.

Imbedded in this remembrance of the Actors' Means Workshop, as we have said, is Proudhammer's recollection of Caleb's return from a vicious Southern prison farm. The recall is triggered for Leo by the physical experience of Madeleine's bed.

I woke up suddenly, out of a sleep like drowning. In my sleep, I had traveled back to Harlem, and I was curled up against Caleb, in our narrow bed. Caleb's chest was hot and heavy. . . . Madeleine's head was on my chest. . . . Her weight was intolerable, and I hated it. . . . Here I was, in this white cunt's bed; here I was, ready for the slaughter. . . . The air whispered, or I whispered, my brother's name. But nothing, now, forever, could rescue my brother, or me.

Younger brother Leo has, in fact, tried to bring comfort to the weeping, brutalized Caleb through their bodies. "He put his arms around me; it was strange to feel that I was *his* big brother now. And he held me so tightly, or, rather, with such an intensity, that I knew, without knowing that I knew it, how empty his arms had been." Leo vows, with "Caleb's breath in my face, his tears drying on my neck," never to forgive "the world." "Never. Never. Never. I would find some way to make them pay. I would do something one day to at least one bland, stupid, happy white face which would change that face forever. . . . I cursed God from the bottom of my heart, the very bottom of my belly."

Caleb tries to join their father in factory work, but cannot bear the treatment he sees inflicted on his father, and goes to California. The void Leo now feels is expressed in terms of desolation, isolation, and chaos.

There is a fearful splendor in absolute desolation: I had never seen it before this day. Everything seemed scrubbed, scoured, older than the oldest bones, and cleaner. Everything lay beneath a high, high, immaculate sky, and was washed as clean as it could be.

The people, the hill, the dying flowers, the height, the sun, all, all, all, were clean as I was not, as I could never be, and all—all—were as remote from me as they would have been had I been in my grave and had drilled a hole through my tombstone to peep out at the world.

"This was the night that I discovered chaos, or perhaps it was the night chaos discovered me; but it certainly began the most dreadful time of my life, a time I am astounded to have survived." "I hit the streets." "Is There Anybody There? said the traveler" appears to be an appropriate title for the despair centered in Book Two of *Tell Me How Long the Train's Been Gone*. Fats Waller's "saving myself for you" in the epigraph, however, suggests a ray of hope which is present in the realistic, honest love of Barbara and Leo, and which is supplemented, in the following and final book, by the love of Black Christopher.

Book Three, entitled "Black Christopher," opens with lines from a traditional spiritual:

> Mother, take your daughter,
>   father, take your son!
> You better run to the city of refuge,
>   you better run!

The "city of refuge" in the Christian sense is contrasted in this final section of the novel with the city of refuge represented by the new, youthful militancy of Black Christopher (a name suggesting "Black Christ") and his friends. Leo Proudhammer becomes involved with Christopher personally and then, perhaps, politically. This last section of the novel attempts to work out, in ways unique for Baldwin, the relationship of personal pain and pleasure to public commitment and the relationship of the elder, successful artist to the brash, young revolutionary. The warning of the epigraph, "You better run!" is here social, and then personal. "The fire next time" is predicted for the American plague cities Leo Proudhammer reenters while recovering from his heart attack, but the fire, he believes, will most certainly consume him as well.

The section opens with the line "The boy sat on the bed, watching me," and the opening short sketch with the as-yet-unnamed "boy," who proves to be Christopher, ends with "I wondered what I had got myself into." From this ultimately unanswered but relevant question we move, once again, as in the first book of the novel, from the hospital, which famous black actor Leo Proudhammer is about to leave, and from Barbara King's spacious hotel suite, where he is taken, to memories of his earlier life. Again, the most painful memory involves brother Caleb and is approached indirectly through related events and characters. In this section, however, Caleb is to some extent replaced by Christopher, a change that supports the thematic preference for young black militancy over old Negro religion.

The hospital champagne party and the presence of the waiting reporters at the time of Proudhammer's leaving permit Baldwin to philosophize about actors and theater and about fame. The play Proudhammer and his visitors were a part of

was a part of our lives and this meant we were now a part
of each other. There really is a kind of fellowship among
people in the theater and I've never seen it anywhere else,
except among jazz musicians. . . . I think it may be partly
because we're forced, in spite of the preposterous airs we
very often give ourselves, to level with each other.

Proudhammer faces a recuperation free of obliga-
tions, lawyers, agents, producers, TV appearances,
civil-rights speeches, lunches, dinners, gossip colum-
nists, and "predatory reporters." He wonders what he
might find in himself, when there is "no need . . . to
do anything but be myself." "Who was this self? . . .
Was he merely having a hard time breathing beneath
the rags and the rubble of the closets I had not opened
in so long?"

The first clear hint we have in the novel that
Caleb, whose loss Leo has bemoaned throughout his
story, is not dead nor in prison nor sick in a literal
sense, comes as Leo is relaxing in front of the fire in
Barbara's living room. About his prospective trip to
New York and from there to Europe for extended recuperation, he thinks, "I knew that I dreaded seeing
Caleb and his wife and his two children." The fire
becomes dominantly symbolic—of human life, of mar-
tyrs, saints, witches, of purification, of constant un-
changing change, of lynchings and burnings. Leo needs
Caleb, "but the fire raged between us." "What a slimy
gang of creeps and cowards those old church fathers
must have been; and remained; and what was my
brother doing in that company?" With this question, we
understand that Caleb's death, imprisonment, and sickness are figurative. Caleb, in fact, has been "saved"
and is now an upright church member and preacher.

Proudhammer's move from Caleb's to Christopher's beliefs is based on American history, as Proudhammer has experienced and observed it. It is not personally a hopeful move. "I had the choice of perishing

with these doomed [American] people, or of fleeing them, and, in that effort, perishing." He is twenty years older than Christopher, but, he despairingly admits, "not all of my endeavor, not all of the endeavor of so many for so long, had lessened [Christopher's] danger in any degree, or in any way at all sweetened the bitter cup." Even though the changes required to fulfill Christopher's revolutionary optimism "would almost certainly be so violent as to blow Christopher, and me, and all of us, away," yet "I committed myself to Christopher's possibilities." The alternative represented by Caleb is scornfully and vulgarly cast aside. With contempt Leo speculates, "Perhaps God would join us later, when He was convinced that we were on the winning side, then, heaven would pass a civil-rights bill and all of the angels would be equal and all God's children have shoes."

The vulgar dismissal of Caleb's alternative comes mostly in Leo's recalling of an earlier theatrical period of his life, advanced chronologically from the period recalled in Book Two. While Leo is a struggling singing waiter in a Village restaurant, and on the verge of success in a courageous production of Emlyn Williams's *The Corn is Green,* Caleb, saved, upright, and respectable, visits him and shames him into visiting their parents. The indirect approach to this memory is through Proudhammer's remembering his mother's death and funeral, which occurred just after the opening of the play, and through a lengthy recalling of one idyllic night spent by Barbara and Leo on the mountaintop above their summer-theater town.

The first visit with Caleb occurs in the restaurant, "The Island," after hours. Caleb narrates the war experiences that led him to salvation, and preaches to, lectures, and advises Leo. "I did not know, when Caleb walked into The Island on that far-off night, how many ways there were to die, and how few to live." For Leo

feels that "the other Caleb, the raging, laughing, seeking Caleb, the Caleb who moaned and wept, the Caleb
who could be lonely—that other Caleb, my brother,
had been put to death and would never be seen again."

At a later meeting, Caleb actually slaps Leo
when Leo tells him to " 'leave me the fuck alone,' "
and Leo lets all his disappointment pour out.

Once, I wanted to be like you. . . . I would have given anything in the world to be like you. . . . Now I'd rather die
than be like you. I wouldn't be like you and tell all these
lies to all these ignorant people, all these unhappy people,
for anything in the world. . . . That God you talk about,
that miserable white cock-sucker—look at His handiwork,
look! . . . I curse your God, Caleb, I curse Him, from the
bottom of my heart I *curse* Him.

The resolution of the story, such as it is, comes in
the last thirty-five pages and is also interspersed with
flashback in Leo Proudhammer's memory. The rise of
Barbara and Leo to international stardom has been
briefly and not very convincingly summarized by this
time, and we are back at Barbara's fireside. Barbara
has sent Christopher money for an airplane ticket to
come and fetch Leo back to New York, and he
arrives bright-faced and fast-talking. "I watched him,"
Leo says, "watched his big teeth, his big hands, listened
to his laugh. He sounded so free; a way I'd never
sounded: a way I'd never been."

Leo recalls, then, their first and second meetings
and subsequent love affair. His older, established protection gave Christopher freedom.

It was, I must say, very beautiful, and it made up for a
lot: Christopher, lying flat on his belly, reading all the long
afternoon. . . . Christopher ruthlessly dominating his
friends, instructing them in everything from terrorism to
sex. . . . They were teaching me a great deal; made me
wonder where I'd been so long. . . . "We are not going to

walk to the gas ovens," Christopher said, "and we are not going to march to the concentration camps. We have to make the mothers know that."

The "hellish" past that Barbara had previously referred to is now revealed to have been an affair between Barbara and Christopher simultaneous with that between Leo and Christopher. " 'He reminded me of you . . . when we were young,' " Barbara says in her confession. " 'He was you before our choices had been made. Before we'd become—what we've become.' "

The resolution of the novel on a personal basis is that, despite the menacing world, their long separations, their respective affairs, their sometimes ruthless struggling for success, Barbara and Leo have come through with a long-term love relationship. Less satisfying in this novel is the resolution, which we feel the author means to go beyond the personal. Christopher's love for Leo is a kind of expiation, or forgiveness, for the wealthy, famous, older artist's distance from the poverty-ridden streets and persons of his youth.

" 'I really would like . . . to know more than I do about what's going on in the streets,' " says Leo to Christopher as they drive through San Francisco. Christopher gets to the point: " 'You *do* know. You want to know if they still love you in the streets.' " And he tells Leo the truth: " 'We can't afford to trust the white people in this country—we'd have to be crazy if we did. But, naturally, a whole lot of black cats think you might be one of them, and, in a way, you know, you stand to lose just as much as white people stand to lose.' " But the forgiveness comes in his following statement: " 'You're a beautiful cat, Leo, and I love you. You believe me? . . . Then don't let this other shit get you down. That's just the way it is, and that's the way it's going to be for awhile.' "

Beyond the personal assurance (Baldwin readers

cannot help but think back to the repeated musical line of *Another Country:* "Do you love me? Do you love me?"), the conclusion of *Tell Me How Long the Train's Been Gone* does little more than express a kind of disillusioned, shakily-founded hope in the youth of America. When he was well, Leo Proudhammer invested his work, his art, with defunct religious hope and imagery. "I could, I *could*, if I kept the faith, transform my sorrow into life and joy. . . . There is no baptism like the baptism in the theater." Incapacitated, unable to work, forced to remove his makeup, his masks, and his roles, having faced death, Leo Proudhammer now invests a hippie dance with that religious hope and imagery.

It was a rite that I was witnessing. . . . It made me think of rites I had seen in Caleb's church, in many churches, of black feet stomping in the mud of the levee; of rites older than that, in forests irrecoverable. The music drove and drove, into the past—into the future. It sounded like an attempt to make a great hole in the world, and bring up what was buried. And the dancers seemed, nearly, in the flickering, violent light, with their beads flashing, their long hair flying, their robes whirling—or their tight skirts, tight pants signifying—and with the music assaulting them like the last, last trumpet, to be dancing in their grave clothes, raised from the dead.

" 'It's a gas,' " says Christopher, who has brought Leo to witness the ear-splitting dance. " 'And there are some real people here and they're making some very nice things happen.' " And the next day, in the last scene, driving toward the Golden Gate bridge, Christopher says, " 'Guns. . . . We need guns. . . . If you don't want me to keep going under the feet of horses, then I think you got to agree that we need us some guns.' " " 'Yes,' " replies Leo, finally, " 'I see that. . . . But we're outnumbered you know.' " " 'Shit,' " replies Christopher, " 'So were the early Christians.' "

This appears to be a rather clear transformation in Leo Proudhammer to commitment to violent revolution. But there is a final paragraph following this dialogue which seems to undercut and make uncomfortably ambiguous all that has gone before, leaving the reader mystified as to Proudhammer's, and Baldwin's, suggested change of purpose. The final paragraph comes many months or even years after Proudhammer's heart attack. He went to New York, he tells us, then to Europe, then came back and did a movie and a play, and "so found myself, presently, standing in the wings again, waiting for my cue." So perhaps the militancy of Christopher did not permanently alter the life of Leo Proudhammer. The title of the novel, though its meaning and significance are difficult to determine, seems to relate to Proudhammer's sense, and the reader's sense, finally, that something has passed the actor by, that he has waited in the station too long, or that events move faster than the thoughtful man can handle.

Reviewers and critics have rather mercilessly pointed out what they perceive to be flaws and weaknesses in *Tell Me How Long the Train's Been Gone*—cardboard characters, excessive vulgarity, polemical tirades, titles of book divisions and epigraphs and even the novel title not clearly connected with the novel, "errant association" in the order and structure of the flashbacks. Some critics have also pointed to achievements, mostly in the evocation of the narrator's Harlem childhood, including outstanding selected incidents, such as young Leo's subway experiences.[2]

There are other strengths in the book as well, however, particularly for a reader not familiar with previous Baldwin works or with black history. Those strengths are in the development of themes and depictions of events mentioned earlier as familiar to readers of other Baldwin works. First, city and small town are both effectively presented as threatening to black survival and interracial communication. Second, criticism of escape through religion, though somewhat overdone here, makes clear an attitude not uncommon in 1968 among black militants and even moderates. Reaction to the violent outcomes of Martin Luther King's nonviolent protests is everywhere apparent, in the novel as in the world.

Third, art as communication of pain is intriguingly, if incompletely, explored for the black actor-artist. Some of the extensively described theater-world parties, tryouts, scenes, are an exposé of that world from the despised but ambitious black actor's view. More importantly, the art form of acting, which demands community and instant communication to be art, serves Baldwin here, as jazz does in his short story "Sonny's Blues," as a model for people reaching one another while remaining individual.

Fourth, the black artist or intellectual working in a white world (the only theater world available to Proudhammer in his early career days) suffers an inevitable estrangement from both the black world of his childhood left behind and the untrusty white world where his hopes lie. This theme, explored elsewhere in Baldwin's works, is most fully carried to positive (or happy) resolution here. Proudhammer's difficulty is in relating to new black militancy, not to his childhood, and his long affair with Barbara King manages to erode the distrust and fear and disdain felt for something called "the white world."

Fifth, and finally, the love experience with Barbara, while perhaps not gruelingly realistic (some critics have called her too good to be true), is a positive model for outliving one's childhood prejudices and fears, for relating honestly and openly across racial frontiers, for a supportive female-male relationship between two strong and successful and unpossessive people. Whether or not Barbara is too good to be real, she comes as a relief and an inspiration to a reader overwhelmed with modern characters too real to be good.

Baldwin's next novel, *If Beale Street Could Talk,* 1974,[3] is more impressive for what it attempts than for what it achieves. Almost all of Baldwin's works are notable for their strong, sensitively explored female characters; [4] this novel attempts a first-person narration by a nineteen-year-old, uneducated, unmarried black female, Clementine Rivers, known as "Tish." Baldwin's analyses of black family life have not always presented families positive enough to sustain characters through adulthood; here Baldwin shows a family united in love for Tish's unborn child, for Tish, and for her lover, unjustly imprisoned Alonzo (Fonny) Hunt. Elsewhere Baldwin has made extensive use of interracial situations, of positive white characters, of homosexual love affairs; here the only humane white is the lawyer hired for Fonny (and sometimes we wonder about him), and there are no homosexual characters at all. Finally, in *Tell Me How Long the Train's Been Gone* we have seen a vehement rejection of Christianity by Leo Proudhammer; in *If Beale Street Could Talk,* that rejection is made even more vehement through the satirical presentation of Fonny's supposedly Christian mother. In this rather short and simple novel, in other words, Baldwin has extended some of his past concerns to logical (if ineffective) conclusions, and has reacted in other ways to criticism he has received.

Although Baldwin said of the book while it was in progress that it was in nine chapters, one for each month of Tish's pregnancy,[5] the final version of *If Beale Street Could Talk* is not divided into chapters, but into two parts, Part One, "Troubled in My Soul," and Part Two, "Zion." The second part of the novel is short, and contains the hopeful suggestions of Fonny's ultimate release. The epigraph for the novel is from a spiritual: "Mary, Mary, / What you going to name that pretty little baby?" The plot, the characters, the dialogue, are all centered on the unborn child. In Tish's words, "Out of this rage and a steady, somehow triumphant sorrow, my baby was slowly being formed." The title is from W. C. Handy's song about Memphis, "Beale Street Blues." "If Beale Street Could Talk, / If Beale Street could talk, / Married men would have to take their beds and walk."

Narration in Tish's voice is an interesting experiment but is not completely successful because it is not entirely consistent. In a 1972 interview, Baldwin said that "to try to tell a story from the point of view of a pregnant woman is something of a hazard. I tried to avoid it, but she's the only one who can tell the story." [6] Tish is able to tell what she herself has seen and done and felt with great sensitivity and occasional brilliance. She tells of visiting Fonny in jail, of giving her parents, Sharon and Joseph, and her older sister, Ernestine, the news of the baby. She tells of the vituperative scene in which the Hunts—Fonny's parents and two sisters— are invited over to hear the news of the baby and to plan strategy for Fonny's release. Tish can tell effectively of her childhood friendship with Fonny, of their growing love, of their first intercourse and their marriage plans, of how it feels to have a baby kicking inside you.

What Tish cannot tell effectively, the story nevertheless demands that she tell. With the awkward transition, "Joseph and Frank [Fonny's father], as we learn later, have also been sitting in a bar, and this is what happened between them," we go thoroughly into event, conversation, and thought far from Tish's direct knowing, as the two fathers plan thefts to raise money for Fonny. And with the introduction, "Sharon gets to

Puerto Rico on an evening plane. She knows exactly how much money she has, which means that she knows how rapidly she must move against time—which is inexorably moving against her," *we* move both out of Tish's experience and Tish's language to follow her mother, in irrelevant detail, through the attempt to reach the woman who has erroneously accused Fonny of rape.

Tish's narrative language fluctuates radically. She is frequently crude, as in calling Fonny's sister, a "dried up yellow cunt," in describing the Avenue of the Americas as having "all those fucking flags on it," and in saying of the policeman who is apparently out to get Fonny: "He walked the way John Wayne walks, striding out to clean up the universe, and he believed all that shit: a wicked, stupid, infantile motherfucker. Like his heroes, he was kind of pin-headed, heavy gutted, big assed, and his eyes were as blank as George Washington's eyes." She is sometimes simply colloquial, as in describing her and Fonny's locating a loft for rent. "This cat, whose name was Levy, really was going to rent it to us, he wasn't full of shit. . . . He dug people who loved each other."

But, frequently, Tish slips into language much less hers than Baldwin's, as in her philosophizing about men and women:

But that noisy, outward openness of men with each other enables them to deal with the silence and secrecy of women. . . . I suppose that the root of the resentment— a resentment which hides a bottomless terror—has to do with the fact that a woman is tremendously controlled by what the man's imagination makes of her—literally, hour by hour, day by day.

And in some large hunks of polemic in the novel, Baldwin's voice and analysis overpower nineteen-year-old Tish's.

The calendars were full—it would take about a thousand years to try all the people in the American prisons, but the Americans are optimistic and still hope for time—and sympathetic or merely intelligent judges are as rare as snowstorms in the tropics. There was the obscene power and the ferocious enmity of the D. A.'s office.

Anyone with conventional standards of morality will have a hard time seeing the Rivers family as Baldwin evidently intends for the reader to see them, as loving and heroic. Sharon leads the family in celebrating Tish's unwed pregnancy as "a sacrament"; Joseph tells Tish, " 'I'm proud of you.' " While the Hunt daughters are guests in the Rivers home, Tish and Ernestine both call them vulgar names, and Ernestine even spits on them. Joseph and Frank, the two fathers, as well as Ernestine and Tish, casually and consistently steal from their employers. As Joseph explains it,

"That white man, baby, and may his balls shrivel and his asshole rot, he *want* you to be worried about the money. . . . I ain't worried about the money—they ain't got no right to it anyhow, they stole it from us—they ain't never met nobody they didn't lie to and steal from. Well, I can steal, too. *And* rob. How do you think I raised my daughters? Shit."

Anything having to do with the United States system of justice is designed to persecute black people, so therefore anything done to frustrate that system is moral. Unfortunately, some of this unconventional morality operates against other blacks caught in that system, too.

The end of *If Beale Street Could Talk* is not clear. Forty-three words before the end, Fonny is still in jail and the trial has been postponed, with bail set. Tish's, or the baby's, "time has come." But then, suddenly, Fonny, who is a self-trained "Sculptor" is "working on the wood, on the stone, whistling, smiling." "And, from far away, but coming nearer, the baby cries and cries and cries and cries and cries and cries and cries and cries, cries like it meant to wake the dead." This is meant, perhaps, to suggest the birth of the baby, or end of Fonny's imprisonment in the future, or both, or something else. At any rate, given the heroism of the family, we know it will all turn out all right, whatever all right is.

Baldwin's attempts in this novel to go in some new directions, in style and content, are interesting, and, for some readers, effective. For others there are major stumbling blocks to accepting his message of save the world for the children. For the careful reader, Tish's narrative quirks interfere with what she is narrating. For all readers, the Rivers family just does not live up to the pride and faith the author wishes us to have in them.

Some of the lack of control and the anger in the book perhaps is generated by the personal experience Baldwin was dramatizing. "A writer is always more or less in his book. . . . You can say I'm the girl, or the boy or their unborn child," he said about *If Beale Street Could Talk*. More specifically, he wrote from the long experience of attempting to gain the release from prison of a friend, Tony Maynard. Maynard was in Attica Prison in New York State before the prisoner rebellion and deaths which brought Attica to the world's attention. "Part of the key to the book is the prison situation," [7] Baldwin said. Frustration and anger certainly do come through clearly in the novel, even if carefully thought out societal analysis and carefully controlled literary form do not.

Tell Me How Long the Train's Been Gone, 1968, and *If Beale Street Could Talk,* 1974, are in many ways very different. The complexity of the first contrasts with the simplicity of the second. The intellectual, artistic, famous male narrator of the first novel contrasts with the uneducated, plain, female narrator of the second. The public life and political conclusions

of Leo Proudhammer are outgrowths of private experience, while the private world of Tish Rivers and
her family are threatened by the larger social world.
The earlier novel, while difficult, is the better novel,
both in exploring Baldwin conflicts and conclusions and
in creating a story to expose those conflicts and test
those conclusions.

6

"The Communion which is the Theatre": *The Amen Corner*, *Blues for Mister Charlie*, and *One Day, When I Was Lost*

In "Notes for *The Amen Corner*," which preface the published play, James Baldwin speaks of his intent in writing for the theater, a difficult undertaking for any essayist and novelist.

I knew that out of the ritual of the church, historically speaking, comes the act of the theatre, the *communion* which is the theatre. And I knew that what I wanted to do in the theatre was to recreate moments I remembered as a boy preacher, to involve the people, even against their will, to shake them up, and, hopefully, to change them.[1]

In a 1961 essay, Baldwin stated the "real aims" of the theater are "to instruct through terror and pity and delight and love. The only thing we can do now for the tired businessman is to scare the living daylights out of him." [2]

The active, physical community of the theatrical experience involves, educates, and changes an audience more readily and more noticeably than do the essay and novel forms. Such a simple (and not so simple) element as music, threading its way through the novels and short stories, reaching a kind of climax in his latest novel, *Just Above My Head,* can be used to hold the theatrical experience together, and to reach and involve even an audience which has not previously *heard* that music. Such involvement is much less predictable with the novel or short story, where evoking sound depends entirely upon the reader's previous sound experience.

Carleton W. Molette, playwright, drama scholar, and director of play production at Spelman College, Atlanta, has written from the theatrical rather than literary point of view about Baldwin's two published plays: *The Amen Corner,* written in the 1950s, first professionally produced in 1965, and published in 1968; and *Blues for Mister Charlie,* written, produced, and published in 1964. He poses the following questions about the effectiveness of a play from a theater worker's view: "Does it come alive on the stage? Does the action of the play flow smoothly and continuously? Will it hold the attention of the audience? Will it have meaning and worth for the audience?" Dr. Molette concludes that, indeed, his experience with Baldwin's two plays enables him to answer yes to these questions. And he credits Baldwin's success in moving from novel to play form, while other novelists have failed, to his "trust of and . . . reliance upon many other artists." The theater demands that the individual artist turn his creation over to others before it is totally complete.[3]

Considering Baldwin's stated intent and Molette's standards for evaluating, this chapter will look at each of Baldwin's two plays with the following questions in mind. First, how do the plot and the form of the play recreate experience? Second, what techniques are used to make the play "come alive," to involve the audience (or the reader)? Third, beyond involving the audience, what in form and content are designed to shake up the viewer or reader? Finally, what are the meaning and worth of the play; how is the viewing or reading likely to change or affect the audience?

The third Baldwin work to be considered here is

of a somewhat different nature, and somewhat different questions will be asked. *One Day, When I Was Lost* is a scenario, or script for a motion picture, based on Alex Haley's lengthy *The Autobiography of Malcolm X*. In considering this work, one must ask not only about Baldwin's intent and accomplishment but about the extent to which the accomplishment is true to the historical character of Malcolm X and true to the autobiography on which it is based.

The Amen Corner is a better play than its production history or critical attention would seem to indicate. Molette calls it "one of the most successful Afro-American plays that I have seen." [4] Here, Baldwin is directly trying to recreate the ritual of the black church, as he knew it, in the ritual of the theater, while teaching a lesson antithetical to the lesson emanating from the church. The play is powerful. The lesson is somewhat less so.

Baldwin's set is ideally suited to the play's action and message. The "church and home of Margaret Alexander," pastor, are at stage right and stage left respectively. The church, with its "camp chairs" for the congregation, is "dominated by the pulpit" and by an "immense, open Bible," and a "thronelike" chair, both on a platform placed in such a way that a speaker from the pulpit is speaking simultaneously to the congregation on stage and the audience in the theater. Pastor Margaret's apartment, which she shares with her older sister, Odessa, her eighteen-year-old son, David, and later with her returned husband, Luke, is placed on a level below the church, at stage left. The church, Baldwin writes in the stage directions, "should give the impression of dominating the family's living quarters."

Action throughout the play moves from the church to the apartment and back to the church. The opening scene takes place in the church; the closing scene has

Margaret and Odessa leaving the church and returning to the apartment. At key points in the plot, action in the upper, church, level occurs while stage lights also illuminate characters in the apartment. Both church and apartment have doors to the outside world which are used symbolically and literally for entering and exiting.

The plot of the story is relatively simple and is developed in a straightforward, realistic, Ibsenesque form, with no flashbacks or expressionistic revelations. All events that took place before the opening time of the play are revealed through simple exposition.

Margaret Alexander has been pastor of the church for several years. Her son, David, has been, until the time of the play, a well-behaved boy who plays the piano for Sunday school and church. On the particular Sunday morning of Act I, Margaret preaches the sermon upstairs and goes down to her apartment to finish packing for a trip to a Philadelphia church. She wants to take David with her; David tries to avoid going.

Elders of the congregation enter the apartment and are subtly critical of Margaret—of the expense of her trip, of her new Frigidaire, and of her son's behavior. Through their conversation, we discover that David's father is in town, working at a jazz club. With that preparation, Luke, the father, arrives, very ill. We discover, with David, that Margaret took her son and left Luke ten years earlier after the death of their baby daughter. Despite Luke's obviously terminal illness, Margaret ends Act I by leaving for Philadelphia, without David. As she says, "In this home, the Lord comes first. The Lord made me leave that man in there a long time ago because he was a sinner. And the Lord ain't told me to stop doing my work just because he's come the way all sinners come."

Act II occurs late the following Saturday. The

critical murmurings of the church elders are growing louder, fed by the revelation of Margaret's past life and the current behavior of her son. "How come she think she can rule a church when she can't rule her own house," says Brother Boxer, who is peeved with Margaret largely because she has ruled that it would be a sin for him to drive a beer truck.

David and Luke have their only conversation in this act, about their past as a family, about music, and about pain. Broken-down Luke is given a key speech of the play in his advice to David. "Son—don't try to get away from the things that hurt you—sometimes that's all you got. You got to learn to live with those things—and—use them. I've seen people—put themselves through terrible torture—and die—because they was afraid of getting hurt." Later Luke explains his imminent demise as due to lack of love at the crucial time when Margaret left him. "A man can lose a whole lot . . . but he can keep on—he can even die with his head up, hell, as long as he got that one thing. That one thing is *him,* David, who he is inside—and, son, I don't believe no man ever got to that without somebody loved him."

When Margaret returns from Philadelphia to face the restless elders, the wayward son, and the dying husband, she is full of "God-given" justification for her own behavior. In dialogue with Luke, she explains her conversion and her leaving him as "finding a hiding place." Luke sees hiding indeed. "Then that other woman—that funny, fast-talking, fiery little thing I used to hold in my arms—[God] done away with her?" And about their son, he avers, "I ain't going to let you make him safe." To Margaret's attempts to make Luke repent to save his soul, he responds, "I guess I could have told you—it weren't *my* soul we been trying to save." Act II ends with the elders gathering up in the church for a business meeting to consider her dismissal, while Margaret, below in her kitchen, weeps and prays "Lord, help us to stand. . . . Lord, give me strength!"

Act III opens with Margaret mounting to the church early the following morning. There she converses with a minor character, but an important alter ego, Mrs. Jackson, who has come from the hospital where her baby has died in great pain. In the church service of Act I, Mrs. Jackson had come forward to ask for prayers for her sick child. At that time, Margaret, questioning the young woman as to why her husband wasn't with her, said, "Maybe the Lord wants you to leave that man." Now Margaret's view has begun to change. To the woman's fear of having more babies, the fear of going through more pain, Margaret says, "That ain't right. That ain't right." And, finally, Margaret advises her to "get on home to your husband. Go on home to your man."

Margaret returns downstairs, while the elders meet above to clinch her ouster. In conversation with David, who comes home drunk, she reveals her protective motivation for seeking his "salvation." "I remember boys like you down home, David, many years ago—fine young men, proud as horses, and I seen what happened to them. I seen them go down, David. . . ." But David refuses further protection. "Mamma, I want to be a man. It's time you let me be a man. You got to let me go."

In the pain of David's leaving and the remembering of her past love for Luke, Margaret says to Odessa:

I tried to put my treasure in heaven where couldn't nothing get at it and take it away from me and leave me alone. . . . I didn't expect that none of this would ever rise to hurt me no more. . . . And there it stand, my whole life, just like I hadn't never gone nowhere. It's an awful thing to think about, the way love never dies!

(This last line, Baldwin says, is the first line he wrote for the play.) Finally, Margaret goes to Luke and they embrace, with the congregation singing above. "I never stopped loving you, Luke. I tried. But I never stopped loving you," she says. And Luke dies.

Margaret ascends to the church and begins a standard sermon, but breaks off in confusion when she realizes she is holding Luke's trombone mouthpiece in her hand, picked up from where he dropped it in death. As the backbiting Sister Moore cries, "Look at her! the gift of God has left her," Margaret speaks with what Baldwin certainly intends to be God's true message:

Children. I'm just now finding out what it means to love the Lord. It ain't all in the singing and the shouting. It ain't all in the reading of the Bible. . . . It ain't even . . . in running all over everybody trying to get to heaven. To love the Lord is to love all His children—all of them, every-one!—and suffer with them and rejoice with them and never count the cost!

Margaret leaves the church. The lights dim on the church and come up on Margaret, below, falling beside Luke's bed.

Baldwin tells us in his notes to *The Amen Corner* that he wrote the play after publishing *Go Tell It on the the Mountain,* and wrote it over the protests of his literary agent. "I remember [it] as a desperate and even rather irresponsible act." As *Go Tell It on the Mountain* in many respects came out of his relation-ship to his father, *The Amen Corner* grew from con-sideration of what motivated his mother, considera-tion of "the strategems she was forced to use to save her children from the destruction awaiting them just outside her door." When we ask how this personal but infinitely duplicated experience is recreated in dramatic form in *The Amen Corner,* we will have to say that the tensions of pain and refuge, acceptance of the physical and seeking of the spiritual are certainly the core of the play, expressed in everything from the Luke-Margaret dichotomy to the jazz-spiritual dichotomy.

But the church, even as protection from the streets, is not given any positive characteristics here; its depiction is much less balanced than it was in *Go Tell It on the Mountain*. The scales of judgement are heavily loaded in favor of worldly love and family rather than congregational communion. No member of the congregation is admirable for any reason. Most are despicable—sex-starved, ambitious, jealous, cruel. This unbalanced view of the church is the greatest weakness in the play. A realistic treatment of any church would likely find at least as much virtue or kindness or love or fellowship there as in other human institutions.

As in other weighted attacks on the church after *Go Tell It on the Mountain*—in *Tell Me How Long the Train's Been Gone* and *If Beale Street Could Talk,* for example—the very vehemence of Baldwin's assaults undercuts his criticism. When one asks how the play recreates experience, one is led to think that it recreates external experience less than it tries to exorcise the power of Baldwin's early religious training.

Despite this lack of balance in the forces set against each other, however, the play is certainly constructed in such a way as to truly "come alive" on the stage. Much of that liveliness and power to involve is transmitted through the music. Group singing, individual singing, instrumental accompaniment, jazz (Luke on record), all provide choral commentary on character and conflict. The rhythms of the Bible readings, the sermons, and the antiphonal phrases—"Praise the Lord!" "Amen!"—are bound to arouse audience reaction.

As to elements of the play designed to "shake up" a viewer or reader, that will largely depend upon the audience. Darwin Turner in "James Baldwin in the Dilemma of the Black Dramatist" concludes that *The Amen Corner* is unselfconsciously written for a black audience, much as later "Black Arts literature" is written consciously for a black audience. Baldwin's "presumption that his audience required no interpretation, no modification, because it already knew the cultural setting," gave him "an artistic freedom rarely granted a black dramatist except when he works within the theater of a black community," Turner says.[5]

If this is so, and it certainly seems to be, the shock to a 1950s black audience would have been the attack on the black church, for even those unaccustomed to believing in it at that time were not accustomed to seeing its conventions so directly contradicted. Shock to later black audiences, in the 1960s, when it was professionally produced, or the 1970s was likely much less. As to most white audiences, were they to have seen the play in the 1950s or were they to see it in the 1980s, they would probably be startled chiefly by the liveliness of the black church service.

What are the meaning and worth of *The Amen Corner*, and how is viewing or reading it likely to change or affect the audience? The meaning is clear in Luke's advice not to avoid pain, but to use it, in Margaret's realization that love never dies, and in her choosing to comfort a dying man she loves down below rather than fight for her job as superior, more-holy pastor above. Such insight is likely to influence a viewer or reader only if he or she is a member of an organized church. If so, the member of the audience could question the form and content of belief, the motive and impact of action. The nonchurch member is less likely to change in word or deed and is more likely to be confirmed in the suspicion that the organized church is the refuge of the self-righteous and the frigid and the cowardly.

Turning to the later play, *Blues for Mister Charlie,* and comparing it to *The Amen Corner,* one finds
a series of differences in form and content and similarity largely in the use of music, again, to involve
the audience. *Blues for Mister Charlie* is expressionistic rather than realistic, and it is much more a protest
play, with a white audience in the author's mind. It is
designed to shock and change the audience, particularly by warning. The period in which it was written,
and the American historical events it makes use of, date
it to a certain extent. Nevertheless, it remains a powerful educational device, particularly for readers and
viewers who are not familiar with the 1960s.

Expressionism in dramatic form may differ from
realism in what appears on the stage. A realistic play
like *The Amen Corner* has a solid set with an actual
Frigidaire, table, chairs, pulpit present on the stage,
giving the viewers the feeling that they are looking at
actual rooms with the fourth wall removed. The expressionistic set which Baldwin uses in his second play,
on the other hand, exists much more by suggestion.

In *Blues for Mister Charlie,* Baldwin describes the
stage set as multiple, with the "skeleton being the
Negro church in the first two acts and the courthouse
in the third." The powerful symbols of the cross and
the flag are continuously visible.

The church and the courthouse are on opposite sides of a
southern street; the audience should always be aware,
during the first two acts, of the dome of the courthouse
and the American flag. During the final act, the audience
should always be aware of the steeple of the church, and
the cross.[6]

Props on stage serve dual function to fit the change
of set from church to courthouse. The pulpit of the first
two acts, placed downstage at an angle, "so that the
minister is simultaneously addressing the congregation

and the audience," becomes in the third act the witness stand of the courthouse.

The aisle of the church "also functions as the division between WHITETOWN and BLACKTOWN." Other scenes such as Richard's room, Lyle's store, Papa D.'s jukebox joint, Jo's kitchen "are to exist principally by suggestion," and appear on the black or the white side of town according to whether the characters are black or white. Additionally, Baldwin says:

for the murder scene, the aisle functions as a gulf. The stage should be built out, so that the audience reacts to the enormity of this gulf, and so that RICHARD, when he falls, falls out of sight of the audience, like a stone, into the pit.

Blues for Mister Charlie does not follow a straight chronology of events. It opens frighteningly, in the dark of the theater, with a gunshot. As lights come up on stage, Lyle Britten, a Southern, white store owner, is seen disposing of a body of a young black man. "And may every nigger like this nigger end like this nigger—face down in the weeds!" he cries.

The rest of the play goes both backward and forward from this opening scene. It goes backward to show the dead, young black man, Richard Henry, returning home from up North, where he has been both a successful singer and a drug addict. It shows his inability to adjust to the racial realities of the Southern town of his birth. He is not humble, soft-spoken, or discreet, and he inevitably gets into trouble with Lyle Britten and his wife, Jo, who are representative of white townspeople who can't imagine what has gone wrong with all the "good niggers" they grew up with.

For the town has been in the throes of typical, early-1960s demonstrations, in support of integration of public facilities. Students from the local college have for months met in the black church run by Reverend

Meridian Henry, Richard's father, and have gone out from their training in nonviolence to demonstrate peacefully, to get spat on, to get beaten up, to be jailed, to be released, and to go out again. Blacktown and Whitetown are exceedingly tense as a result, with rumors of sabotage and fear of sounds in the dark.

Love interest in the plot is provided by one of the demonstrating students, Juanita, who was a childhood friend of Richard Henry. She has been pursued unsuccessfully by another student, Pete; by Reverend Henry, who lost his wife years earlier; and by Parnell James, the wealthy, white, liberal, newspaper editor. When Richard returns, Juanita and Richard realize and consummate their love, and Richard is on the path to a new life and new goals when he is shot by Britten.

Throughout the rest of the play the events leading up to the opening murder scene are interspersed with events following the murder. Parnell James, although a good friend of Lyle Britten, succeeds in gaining Lyle's arrest for the murder of Richard Henry. Lyle is put on trial and is ultimately, predictably, acquitted. On the witness stand, black and white witnesses alike lie, and, in nonrealistic fashion, the thoughts and reactions of Blacktown and Whitetown are expressed in chorus. As witnesses testify, the audience sees not only their lies but glimpses, through their expressed memories, the histories which explain their testimonies.

The overriding question of *Blues for Mister Charlie,* perhaps more relevant for the black liberation movement in 1964 than in 1980, is the individual and communal debate over nonviolent protest versus "freedom by any means necessary." The dominant symbol for "any means necessary" is the gun. Much is made by the state prosecutor, when Parnell James is on the witness stand, of the fact that Parnell has hunted frequently with white Lyle Britten, his avowed friend, but has never hunted with black Meridian Henry, also his avowed friend. "Is it not true, Mr. James," he is questioned, "that it is impossible for any two people to go on a hunting trip together if either of them has any reason at all to distrust the other?"

Whitetown is of course armed; Blacktown is not. Richard Henry brings a gun with him when he returns home from the North, but he turns it over to his father when he begins to see a new life ahead with Juanita. After the murder of Richard and the acquittal of his murderer, Reverend Meridian Henry (the very name suggests a moderate, or middle, view), changes his mind. In Act 1, as Meridian begins to question events, Parnell admonishes him, "Meridian, you can't be the man who gives the signal for the holocaust." Meridian asks in response: "Must I be the man who watches while his people are beaten, chained, starved, clubbed, butchered?" At the end of the play, Meridian says, "You know, for us, it all began with the Bible and the gun. Maybe it will end with the Bible and the gun." "What did you do with the gun, Meridian?" asks Juanita. It is "in the pulpit," Meridian replies, "under the Bible. Like the pilgrims of old."

Within this overriding question of appropriate or moral means to desired ends, other issues are explored. For example, what is the role of the white liberal in racial struggle? Parnell is the only character who communicates with both sides, the only character who even wishes to do so. Yet he is not totally heroic. On the witness stand, he cannot bring himself to expose white woman Jo Britten's lie that Richard Henry tried to rape her, even though he knows it is a lie.

At the end of the play, as Blacktown gathers to march once again, Parnell asks Juanita, "Can I join you on the march, Juanita? Can I walk with you?" Juanita replies "Well, we can walk in the same direction;

work toward the same goals; but work in your own community." This advice to the white liberal in 1964 predates by a year or two the Black Power movement, which sought to remove whites from powerful positions in civil rights organizations. Racism is not essentially a black problem; it is a white problem. As Malcolm X advised, so suggests Baldwin: walk in the same direction; work in your own community.

Another issue explored, the one, Baldwin says, which forced him to write the play, is trying to understand how a man like Lyle Britten can do what he does —kill. The "germ of the play" for Baldwin was in the murder of fifteen-year-old Emmett Till in 1955 in Mississippi. Till was a young, Northern black who whistled at a white woman and consequently was killed. His murderer was acquitted. "I do not know *why* the case pressed on my mind so hard," Baldwin says in his prefatory "Notes for *Blues for Mister Charlie.*" "In life, obviously, such people baffle and terrify me and, with one part of my mind at least, I hate them and would be willing to kill them."

But Baldwin goes on, in a statement that forms the key to the depiction of the white characters in the play,

Yet, with another part of my mind, I am aware that no man is a villain in his own eyes. Something in the man knows—*must* know—that what he is doing is evil; but in order to accept the knowledge the man would have to change. What is ghastly and really almost hopeless in our racial situation now is that the crimes we have committed are so great and so unspeakable that the acceptance of this knowledge would lead, literally, to madness. The human being, then, in order to protect himself, closes his eyes, compulsively repeats his crimes, and enters a spiritual darkness which no one can describe. . . . [But] we have the duty to try to understand this wretched man; and while we probably cannot hope to liberate him, begin working toward the liberation of his children. For we, the American people, have created him, he is our servant. . . . It is we who have locked him in the prison of his color.[7]

In order to help the reader and viewer understand Lyle Britten as he appears to himself rather than simply as a villain, Baldwin shows us the man with his family, with his baby son ("old pisser," as he calls him), and gives us a great deal of Lyle's sexual and racial history. As one would expect in Baldwin, sex and race are closely related in Lyle's history. Lyle's wife, Jo, is given a sympathetic portrayal within the racial and sexual limits of her upbringing. Her lying on the witness stand becomes understandable from her viewpoint.

Let us summarize to this point what we have said about *Blues for Mister Charlie* and answer more directly the question, "How do the plot and the form of the play recreate experience?" The expressionistic form of the play recreates experience very well, for the race attitudes Baldwin is depicting exist in confused, dreamlike form, he is saying, in every American, black or white. The outcomes of the confusion, the prejudices, the fears are historically accurate— marches, beatings, jailings, rapes, killings. Inner and outer experience of a particular time and particular place are powerfully and accurately recreated.

How, then, does the play come alive? Much is done here, as in *The Amen Corner,* with music and with other sounds. The first sound is the terrifying shot in the dark. The next sounds are from the training sessions of withstanding taunts that the demonstrators go through before facing the streets. "Hey, boy, where's your mother? I bet she's lying up in bed, just a-pumping away. . . . You get your ass off these streets from around here, boy, or we going to do us some cutting— we're going to cut that big black thing off of you, you hear?"

Later sounds include Richard singing; Meridian, Juanita, and Peter singing Richard's songs, one about freedom and one about prison; jukebox music and dancing in Papa D.'s joint; menacing car sounds and telephone sounds; Richard's guitar; white folks singing "For He's a Jolly Good Fellow" at Lyle's and Jo's anniversary, while the sounds of Blacktown singing are heard in the background; Jo singing the baby to sleep; the singing at Richard's funeral; Jo's and Lyle's baby crying as Jo takes the witness stand; student demonstrators singing in the jail; journalists' reports in many tongues at Lyle's trial; and again, near the end of the play, as the full story of the killing is replayed, gunshots.

Blues for Mister Charlie is designed to shock the audience, though here, as with *The Amen Corner,* the shock for a white audience and a black audience will be very different. Darwin Turner has said, in "James Baldwin in the Dilemma of the Black Dramatist," that *Blues for Mister Charlie* is written for a white audience," is "patterned on the protest tradition," and "calls upon the Parnells of America to defend their convictions even if such action pits them against their neighbors." [8] Carlton Molette agrees that it is written for a white audience, but explains some of the play's unwieldy complexity as the result of trying "to be all things to all people. It tries to explain whites to blacks and blacks to whites."

Interestingly, Molette describes conversations among blacks and among whites in the theater lobby during intermissions and following *Blues for Mister Charlie*. Whites were mystified by portions of the play blacks understood, and blacks were unable to adjust to Lyle Britten's *not* being portrayed as what they expected or wanted to see—"some kind of wild-eyed, nigger-hating, stereotyped redneck villain." [9] From such reaction it is apparent that Baldwin succeeds in shocking both audiences.

The worth of *Blues for Mister Charlie* lies particularly in raising, recreating, and struggling with questions that have not been resolved in the sixteen years since its writing. Names and datelines and groups change; the questions reoccur. In liberation movements that have followed on the black struggle, which itself has by no means ended, the same positions, the same arguments, the same questions arise. In the women's, Native American, Chicano, immigrant, gay, handicapped liberation movements, at what point are violent action and violent defense necessary? At what point are they inevitable? At what point are they justified? Moral? Productive?

It is easy to forget, when one has lived through a period of history noted for events and debates, that the schools and the courts and the hospitals and the voting booths are continually being repopulated by people who have not lived through the events or the debates. If there is to be learning from the past, the past must be recreated repeatedly. *Blues for Mister Charlie* does a masterful job of recreating. It deserves being produced, viewed and read now, as it did in 1964.

One Day, When I Was Lost [10] is a movie script Baldwin published in 1973, several years after he walked out on a Columbia Pictures contract. The contract was for a film on the life of Malcolm X, to be based on Alex Haley's *The Autobiography of Malcolm X*. In *No Name in the Street,* his 1972 book, Baldwin describes the problems which led him to give up on the Columbia Pictures project, mostly his sense of being pressured into a view of Malcolm X he thought inaccurate.

Malcolm X, whom Baldwin considered a friend

with whom he didn't always agree, began life as Malcolm Little; continued as a pimp, a thief, a hustler; was converted to Islam, the Black Muslim form, while in prison; became the most militant, prominent, and effective spokesperson for black liberation in the country, perhaps in the world; and was assassinated in 1965, as he spoke in the Audubon Ballroom in Harlem.

To convey several of these periods in Malcolm X's life, Baldwin uses, in the scenario, a flashback technique. The script opens with the camera moving "in New York, from the Statue of Liberty in the bay, and the busy water traffic, the downtown spires, the midtown spires, [to] the garage of the New York Hilton Hotel." After a "long, lean" man, with "bespectacled eyes . . . both haunted and alert" enters the garage, gets into a car, and drives out, the car radio announces Malcolm X's appearance that evening at the Audubon Ballroom. Meanwhile, "the sideview mirror begins to reflect inexplicable images, swift, over-lapping, blurred."

The recurring violent images in the sideview mirror are of a Klan raid and fire in Malcolm's youthful home and of the trolley-car tracks where Malcolm's father was pushed to his death. With these images interspersed, the scenario covers parts of Malcolm's life with short, crisp scenes. The last line belongs to Betty, his wife, and is spoken at Malcolm X's funeral: "You are present when you are away." The line serves as a leitmotif for the entire screenplay, and an effective summary of Baldwin's feeling for the significance of Malcolm X's life.

Unless one has an intensely visual imagination, it is difficult to read a screenplay in such a way as to make reading as meaningful as viewing the film would be. The visual techniques Baldwin uses, one can only say, would appear to provide the basis for a very effective film. One must also add, however, that the dis-

covery of Malcolm X, of his life and his ultimate principles of belief and faith, can be made much more
fully and effectively through the reading of Haley's
Autobiography of Malcolm X, which Malcolm X essentially controlled.

Not only does the lengthy autobiography include
more of Malcolm's life and thought, it also covers
incidents in greater and more accurate detail. Patsy
Bremington Perry, in an article on the scenario entitled
"One Day, When I Was Lost: Baldwin's Unfulfilled
Obligation," summarizes the history of Baldwin's writing of the screenplay and closely compares the resulting
publication with the autobiography on which it is
based. She concludes that "in his inordinate emphasis
on violence in America, in his transformations of
important persons and events; and in his undercutting
of Malcolm's contributions, achievements, and potential for achievement, Baldwin lost much of the tone of
Malcolm's life."

The emphasis on violence, Perry says, gained
through selection, repetition, and addition, not only is
misleading in considering the whole of Malcolm's life,
but results in the impact of the screenplay being protest
rather than information. Transformations of persons
and events include absence of Malcolm's family, his
sister, Ella, for example, and his brother, Reginald,
who introduced Malcolm to Elijah Muhammad's version of Islam. Transformations provide other characters
as substitutes for real-life people from the *Autobiography of Malcolm X*. A fictitious prisoner named
Luther, for example, introduces Malcolm to the Black
Muslim faith, and is also, out of prison, the second-in-
command to whom Malcolm is subordinate. Many
words which were actually spoken by Elijah Muhammad are put by Baldwin into the mouth of Luther. In
real life, Malcolm was second-in-command to Elijah
Muhammad. Even in such detail as the creation of the

Black Muslim newspaper, *Muhammad Speaks,* Malcolm X, who created it, is given only half the credit as creating it jointly with another person in the screenplay. Malcolm X is presented, Perry says, misleadingly, with "shriveled powers." [11]

One has the feeling that it was probably a mistake for Baldwin to attempt a project controlled by the studio initially, and then, after he dropped the studio contract, by the necessity of historical and literary accuracy in relation to the autobiography. Baldwin's urge to make in the screenplay his own protest and statement about American violence as a determinant of Malcolm X's career overwhelms the fuller statement that was already there in *The Autobiography of Malcolm X.* It would be interesting, however, to see Baldwin attempt a screenplay of his own life or fiction, given the skill with which he handles the form.

In a 1979 interview at the time of the publication of *Just Above My Head,* his most recent novel, Baldwin indicated that he is planning to return to writing or producing for the theater. Given the memorable power of his two published plays and the promise of his single scenario,[12] the reader and viewer can only hope that he develops those plans.

7

Charting Racism in America, 1945-1965:

Going to Meet the Man

James Baldwin's short stories, most of which have been collected in the 1965 publication, *Going to Meet the Man,* are expression, in miniature, of ideas and themes explored elsewhere in novels, essays, and plays. Daryl Dance's very useful bibliographical essay, "James Baldwin," in *Black American Writers: Bibliographical Essays,* Volume 2,[1] lists uncollected stories that also appear as chapters of Baldwin's novels or plays; and "Death of a Prophet," which appeared in *Commentary* in 1950, closely parallels the autobiographical description of his father's death in Baldwin's essay "Notes of a Native Son." Only the eight stories appearing in the 1965 collection, *Going to Meet the Man,* will be examined here.

It is instructive to look at the stories in the order in which Baldwin and his editors placed them in *Going to Meet the Man,* an order that is close to but not identical with the order in which they were first written and/or published. More importantly, the order allows us to explore character from youth to middle life, and offers a form of historical chart of racism in America from 1954 to 1965.

The first two stories in the collection, "The Rockpile," first published with the collection in 1965, and "The Outing," first published in *New Story* in 1951, bear much resemblance in character, event, and theme to *Go Tell It on the Mountain*. "The Rockpile" concerns a day in the life of essentially the same family and community that appear in the novel: John, stepson of Gabriel, the husband of his mother, Elizabeth; younger brother, Roy; Aunt Florence; Sister McCandless. The event of the story is much like the scene in the novel in which Roy has been in a fight with white boys and has been cut above the eye. In "The Rockpile," however, the locus of the fight is directly across the street from the family's tenement apartment, on a "mass of natural rock jutting out of the ground," and is not with white boys but with Roy's neighborhood friends.

Roy, forbidden to leave the house, nevertheless sneaks out on a Saturday with John's knowledge and is hurt on the rock pile. As he is being tended by his mother, Elizabeth, and visiting Sister McCandless, Gabriel arrives home, kneels in concern at Roy's side, scolds Elizabeth, and is about to beat Johnnie, who is protected by Elizabeth. The story ends with John ordered to pick up his father's lunchbox from the floor. Elizabeth "heard, behind her, his scrambling movement as he left the easy chair, the scrape and jangle of the lunchbox as he picked it up, bending his dark head near the toe of his father's heavy shoe."

The last line of the story evidently alludes to the words of God to the serpent in the Garden of Eden after the Fall of Adam and Eve: "I will make you enemies of each other: you and the woman, your offspring and her offspring. It will crush your head and you will strike its heel." The theme of the story lies in what is to come after its conclusion, in other words, in the hatred that will somehow be returned to Gabriel from his stepson.

The differences between "The Rockpile" and the similar incident in *Go Tell It on the Mountain* are significant. In the novel, Roy has gone across town to fight with white boys, yet Gabriel blames the white boys. In the novel, John has no responsibility for Roy's action. In the novel, Roy curses his father, after Gabriel attacks Elizabeth, and Roy receives the beating. The irony of the favored and true son being incorrigible and hating his father, in other words, is used to full advantage in the context of the novel. The short story, on the other hand, provides little explanation of the enmity between the stepson and stepfather.

One episode in "The Rockpile" is used also in *Another Country*—the drowning of a boy in the "garbage-heavy" Harlem River. The descriptions are very similar, though the uses to which they are put differ. In the short story, the drowning represents to Elizabeth and her sons the dangers they must be protected from on the streets. In the novel, the incident, part of Rufus Scott's recollection of his youth, is more integrated with Rufus's tortured memory and his ultimate death by drowning.

"The Outing," the second story in *Going to Meet the Man,* also has John and Roy and Gabriel and Elizabeth as central characters. David, a friend somewhat older than John, a character not in *Go Tell It on the Mountain,* appears here also. John is somewhat older than he is in "The Rockpile" or in the novel. The three boys, John, Roy, David, all beginning to be actively interested in sexual involvement, journey with a church group up the Hudson River to Bear Mountain for a one-day outing.

Roy and David are interested in girls, Roy particularly in a girl named Elizabeth, David in a girl named Sylvia. The three boys have purchased a butterfly pin for Sylvia's birthday and throughout the day try to find Sylvia apart from her mother and from Brother Elisha, self-appointed protectors of the girl, so they can give her the pin. John, while this is going on, discovers that his real interest is in David, not in Sylvia or in any other girl.

The discovery makes his and David's friendship new and menacing, and David's interest in Sylvia a new source of jealousy. Early in the trip, John and David have "mounted to the topmost deck" of the boat, where "the air was sharp and clean. They faced the water, their arms around each other." John "buried his face in David's shoulder," as David whispers, " 'Who do you love? . . . Who's your boy?' " "You,' " John mutters "fiercely, 'I love you.' "

Later, on the way home, again on the top deck, "Johnnie moved and put his head on David's shoulder. David put his arms around him. But now where there had been peace there was only panic and where there had been safety, danger, like a flower, opened."

The saints' emotional, physical shouting service and the juxtaposition of need for "salvation" with developing sexuality are linked more fully and effectively in *Go Tell It on the Mountain* than in this short story. Again, as with "The Rockpile," the story uses characters and incidents more fully integrated in the novel. The story does, however, make the discovery of homosexual love more important than the novel does. The title, "The Outing," suggests "coming out," the admission of homosexuality, even though in the story itself John "comes out" only to himself. This sensitive portrayal of a young boy's own discovery of his homosexual interest is important for its date of publication: 1951. Later Baldwin novels, particularly *Another Country* and *Just Above My Head,* go further in showing in detail the early development and discovery of that interest.

The third story in *Going to Meet the Man* seems at first out of place in the collection and out of character for Baldwin. Called "The Man Child," it tells the tale of a white farm family—Eric, an eight-year-old blond boy, Eric's father, and Eric's mother—and their friend, the father's war buddy, Jamie. Eric's father has inherited *his* father's land and has taken over Jamie's inherited land, too. Eric's father has a wife and little boy; Jamie has neither. And Eric's father makes very sure that Eric and Jamie both know what Eric will inherit and what Jamie will never have.

A bit of Jamie's submerged bitterness comes out at the birthday party he is paternalistically given by Eric's father and mother, but the accumulated, silent resentments only emerge at the end of the story, surprising the innocent Eric and the innocent reader. Jamie lures Eric into the barn and slowly breaks his neck. Eric, meanwhile, to no avail, promises Jamie " 'I'll be your little boy forever and forever and forever—and you can have all the land and you can live forever!' "

The story is allegorical. Jamie, the dispossessed, strikes back to kill, to make sure no one possesses what he has been deprived of. " 'This land . . . will belong to no one,' " he answers Eric's promises. And at the end, after the murder, Jamie walks out of his house and "down the road, his dog beside him, his hands in his pockets," the eternal wanderer.

The story at first seems out of place and character because of the absence of racial or sexual explorations. But when seen as essentially allegorical, a story of dispossession, particularly dispossession of land, and a story of revenge, it makes sense as a Baldwin story placed where it is in the collection of stories.

The title can refer to any of the male actors in the historical drama. It can refer to Eric's father, adult male possessor of land, woman, and child, who childishly fails to recognize accumulating frustration and resentment in another adult male, treating him like a child. It can refer to Eric, the "manchild in the prom-

ised land," who stands to inherit everything, but in ac-
tuality inherits accumulated hatred of whose cause he
is innocent, and who receives not wealth, but death. Or
finally, it can refer to Jamie, the man treated and even
named like a child, who can only lash out like a child,
whose power is destructive, since he has been denied
access to positive power. In any case, or in all cases,
the warning of "The Man Child" as allegory is clear.

"Previous Condition," the following story, first
published in *Commentary,* is another story about dispossession. This story is not so much allegorical, however, as painfully realistic, particularly for the date of
its writing, 1948. The story is told in the first person by
an unemployed black actor who left his New Jersey home at age sixteen to travel all over the United
States and to work at "just about everything." "I hated
all the people in my neighborhood," he says about his
youth. "They went to church and they got drunk. They
were nice to the white people. When the landlord came
around they paid him and took his crap."

Peter, our narrator, however, has not gotten much
further. As the story opens, he is shakily living in a
room where Negroes are not allowed, rented for him
by a "Jewboy" friend, Jules. The landlady of course
discovers him and kicks him out, and he, despite urg-
ings of Jules and a "shanty Irish" female friend, Ida,
puts up no fight. He has learned "how to get by."

Early images of the story suggest on-going torture.
When Peter wakes up, "the sheet was gray and twisted
like a rope. I breathed like I had been running. I
couldn't move for the longest while. I just lay on my
back, spread-eagled. . . ." [2] The walls of the room are
the "color of chipped dry blood."

After Peter is kicked out of the room, he wanders to Jules's apartment and then has dinner with Ida.
Neither sympathetic friend can understand, or know,

his reactions and feelings. Finally, he gets on a subway train full of "anonymous, islanded people . . . behind make-up, fat, fleshy masks and flat eyes," and ends up in a rundown Seventh Avenue bar in Harlem. "God save the American republic" he repeats here, as he did earlier downtown.

Not at home and roomless downtown, he is no more at home here. "I longed for some opening, some sign, something to make me a part of the life around me. But there was nothing except my color. . . . I didn't seem to have a place." Even when an opening is breached by an older woman for whom he has bought a drink, he cannot respond. " 'Baby,' " she says, " 'what's your story?' " " 'I got no story, Ma,' I said," is the concluding line.

The theme of the story is an expansion of the earlier dispossession story, for it explores the dual-dispossession of the black artist or intellectual, not fully understood among white liberal friends, not at home any longer in Harlem bars nor in his childhood world. Some of the lines, the memories, of Leo Proud-hammer, actor-narrator of *Tell Me How Long the Train's Been Gone,* are similar in describing that isola-tion between two worlds, his belonging in neither. "My life, in effect, had not yet happened in anybody's con-sciousness," remembers Proudhammer about his first fringe-of-the-theater jobs. "Sometimes, alone, I fled to the Negro part of town. . . . But my connections all were broken."

"Previous Condition" does not, however, as the novel does, suggest resolution to this conflict or isola-tion. The allusion of the title is probably to the Fif-teenth Amendment to the Constitution of the United States: "The right of citizens of the United States to vote shall not be denied or abridged by the United States or by any State on account of race, color, or previous condition of servitude." The allusion suggests that, in fact, the "previous condition of servitude" continues unabated for Peter and other dispossessed and embittered blacks.

The next two stories in *Going to Meet the Man,* "Sonny's Blues," first published in *Partisan Review* in 1957, and "This Morning, This Evening, So Soon," from the *Atlantic Monthly,* 1960, are the longest of Baldwin's stories, and the ones, also, that have received the most critical attention and have been most frequently anthologized.

"Sonny's Blues," as the title suggests, makes use of the function, form, and impact of the blues to convey its point about individual and community identity. The first person narrator of the story, a struggling, straight, Negro schoolteacher, tells the story of his younger brother from his youth to his arrest on drug charges and ultimately to his release after treatment. It is the pain of the death of his young daughter that moves the teacher to make contact with his brother. "My trouble made his real." It is the younger brother's piano playing, finally, that reaches the older brother with a communication of pain and vision and community.

After the death of their parents, the older brother, home on emergency leave from the army, asks Sonny what he wants to do. " 'I want to play jazz,' " Sonny replies. "I simply couldn't see why on earth he'd want to spend his time hanging around nightclubs, clowning around on bandstands, while people pushed each other around on a dance floor," remembers the narrator. But at the end of the story, as Sonny brings his brother into his jazz-club world, the older brother begins to learn from the younger what the menace, the pain, the escape of drugs have meant for Sonny. The pain, the feeling, are transformed into blues. "Creole," the bass player, began to tell us what the blues were all about. They were not about anything very new. He and his boys up there were keeping it new, at the risk of ruin, destruction, madness, and death, in order to find new ways to make us listen. For while the tale of how we suffer, and how we are delighted, and how we may triumph is never new, it always must be heard. There isn't any other tale to tell, it's the only light we've got in all this darkness.

When Sonny plays, his brother realizes that "freedom lurked around us and I understand, at last, that he could help us be free if we would listen, that he would never be free until we did." Sonny leads his brother into "a discovery of self in community," by means of the blues, a "combination of personal and social significance in a lyric encounter with history." [3] Art can be a means for release from the "previous condition" when it is heard, listened to, understood.

"This Morning, This Evening, So Soon" takes us a bit further along the historical progression the stories skim, to the early 1960s, with integration in the United States progressing slowly under increasing pressure from activist civil rights leaders.[4] We view the changes with some doubt through the eyes of an unnamed, famous black actor about to return "home" to the United States for a tour, with his Swedish wife and young French-born son, after twelve years in France.

John V. Hagopian, in "James Baldwin: the Black and the Red-White-and-Blue," accurately describes the sections of the story as "Family," "Friend," and "Stranger." "It moves from the intimate center of the unnamed narrator's experiences outward into public life and society." [5] The story begins in the Parisian home of the narrator, his wife, son, and visiting black sister. It subsequently moves outward to include Vidal, the director of the film by which the narrator has gained his fame, and then to a group of traveling black

American students whom the narrator and director meet and befriend in a bar.

The narrator's fear of return to the United States, expressed with a controlling image of nightmares, is centered upon what the experience will mean for his young son, who is as yet unexposed to racial slurs and racist actions. The invasion of the public into the private is intensified by race and by fame. "For everyone's life begins on a level where races, armies, and churches stop. And yet everyone's life is always shaped by races, churches, and armies; races, churches, armies menace, and have taken, many lives."

Falling in love with Harriet, "on a bridge, one tremendous, April morning" was, the narrator recalls, his first experience of being along with someone, without the menacing world.

Never, in all my life, until that moment, had I been alone with anyone. The world had always been with us, between us, defeating the quarrel we could not achieve, and making love impossible. During all the years of my life, I had carried the menacing, the hostile, killing world with me everywhere . . . —that world which I had learned to distrust almost as soon as I learned my name, that world on which I knew one could never turn one's back, the white man's world.

When he had briefly returned to New York for his mother's funeral, he found that he "had forgotten all the tricks on which my life had once depended." The necessity, now, of refamiliarizing himself with those "tricks," and, worse yet, of teaching them to his son, terrifies him. It is Vidal's questions of "How will you raise your son? Will you teach him never to tell the truth to anyone?" that have helped the narrator to perform the film role of Chico, son of a Martinique woman and French colonialist.

The past suffering of the Jewish Vidal, the experiences, negative and positive, of the black American students, and the suffering and reactions of Boona, a despised Tunisian thief, all bring the narrator around to a more optimistic view of his place in the world and his relationship to it. He returns to his home and picks up his son early on the dawn of a new day. " 'I feel very cheerful, I do not know why,' " he says. Madame Dumont, who has cared for the son, exclaims " 'Ah, . . . you are going on a journey! . . . What a journey! *Jus qu'au nouveau monde!*' 'Yes,' I say, all the way to the new world.' I press the button and the cage, holding my son and me, goes up."

John Hagopian says that "the symbolism of the ending is clear." Caged in their Negro skins, the narrator and son are nevertheless "rising in the world." The narrator has discovered through the night of moving out from family to friend to stranger that "his original feeling that everything was divided into his oppressed self and the hostile world was false, that he is a part of a history and a humanity that is far more complex than that." [6] "This Morning, This Evening, So Soon," provides an outstanding depiction of American racial experience and expatriation from a worldwide perspective, an outstanding melding of the personal dream with the public nightmare.

The penultimate story of Baldwin's short story collection, "Come Out the Wilderness," first appeared in *Mademoiselle* in 1958. It supplements the other stories in several interesting ways: in being told in third-person, limited narration from a black woman's point of view; in dealing with integration from the view of a token integrator; in exploring the problem of a heterosexual, interracial experience at the time of its writing.

Twenty-six-year-old Ruth, the central character, has been living with a white man, Paul, but at the time of the story is certain that he is preparing to leave her. She loves him deeply and sees a beauty in him that other people do not see—"it was like thinking that the sun was ordinary." They are not married, and she cannot help feeling that he treats her cavalierly "because she was a colored girl"; consequently, Ruth will not place demands upon him or even show her concern at his behavior.

Ruth works in a downtown insurance company, a token black secretary. The handsome, single, black manager, Mr. Davis, asks her to become his personal secretary, takes her to lunch, and talks to her, but there is no clear suggestion at the end of the story that this prospective association will compensate for the love lost, the love failed, between Paul and Ruth. She walks out into the rain, at the end of the story, hiding from the crowds and "from herself the fact that she did not know where she was going."

Baldwin's narration of sexual experience as well as career experience through a black woman's perception works well in this story. Ruth's frustration goes back to the treatment she received from her brother and father when she was seventeen and was discovered "alone in a barn with a boy." Nothing had taken place between the two, but the brother and father leapt to conclusions and beat both Ruth and the boy. Her brother's words: " 'You dirty . . . you dirty . . . you black and dirty!" follow her to the city and thread through all her relationships. "And she felt dirty, she felt that nothing would ever make her clean."

Paul's arms, Paul's love cannot release her from this sense of dirt, apparently because of his own racial past and guilt. "Whenever he touched her, she became blacker and dirtier than ever; the loneliest place under heaven was in Paul's arms." Near the conclusion of the story, as Ruth tries to sort through and understand what has happened to her, to her loves, she recognizes that "the sons of the masters were roaming the world, looking for arms to hold them. And the arms that might have held them—could not forgive."

We have in the story another case of dispossession, of intrusion of the menacing world, this time on a black woman, and at a more recent period of time, when external discrimination has been replaced by internalized self-hatred, both in the white and black actors of the personal and historical drama.

The final story of *Going to Meet the Man,* is the title story, first published with the collected stories in 1965. We have moved from the youthful characters of the early stories to a middle-aged man as central character. We have moved historically to the mid-sixties, to mid-civil rights nonviolent protests throughout the South. We have also moved from exploring what racism in the United States has done to youngsters, black intellectuals and artists, black women, to what it has done to a Southern white male, to "the man," whose previously stable world is daily changing around him.

The central character of "Going to Meet the Man" is a white, forty-two-year-old sheriff's deputy, Jesse, whose role demands that he subdue Negro voter-registration demonstrators in his small Southern town. The unanticipated courage, singing, and resistance of the demonstrators has forced him and his fellow lawmen to use ever-increasing cruelties and violence, including electric cattle prods, on the incarcerated demonstration leaders.

The plot of the story is simple. " 'What's the matter?' " is the first line, and it is asked by his wife, Grace, as the two lie in bed, frustrated by his impotence. The story then explores in flashback just what is the matter, by describing his day with the demonstrators and then his earlier life. The crucial event of his childhood was an incredible picnic-lynching-burning of a black man, an event to which he was escorted gaily by his parents and their friends. After he has recalled that event in detail, he turns to make successful "love" to his wife, crying and laughing, " 'Come on, sugar, I'm going to do you like a nigger, just like a nigger, come on, sugar, and love me just like you'd love a nigger.' "

Jesse is, in a sense, Lyle Britten of *Blues for Mister Charlie* explored in more detail.[7] Baldwin is asking here, as he did in the preface to that play, how one can explain the reprehensible actions of another human being as human. How can we understand this man, who would put a cattle prod to a woman's breast, from the inside out?

In Baldwin's understanding, here as elsewhere in essays and novels, sex and violence and color are intermixed irrevocably from early experience onward. Moving back in time with Jesse from the bedroom scene, where his holster lies atop his pants, we remember with him the times he "wanted a little more spice than Grace could give him," when he picked up "a black piece" or arrested her—"it came to the same thing." He goes back further to the men who had been his models, to his father and his father's friends. "They had taught him what it meant to be a man."

The inescapable singing being used in the demonstrations brings Jesse back further to a memory of an eight-year-old coming home in the dark with his father and mother. " 'I guess they singing for him. . . . Even when they're sad, they sound like they just about to go and tear off a piece,' " his father says as he fondles his mother. And hiding under a blanket later, at home, Jesse hears "his mother's moan, his father's sigh," the rocking bed. "His father's breathing seemed to fill the world."

The event which has brought on such lusty action in Jesse's father is the lynching and burning of a black man who has "knocked down" a white woman. The details of the gelding of the man, his burning, his flesh being torn from his body by hands, knives, rocks of the crowd, are excruciatingly but tantalizingly told, just as they exist in excruciating, tantalizing detail in Jesse's memory. The sexual violence of the event leads to a kind of orgasm in the crowd, an orgasm Jesse recognizes in the resultant peaceful, sweaty face of his father. "At that moment Jesse loved his father more than he had ever loved him. He felt that his father had carried him through a mighty test, had revealed to him a great secret which would be the key to his life forever."

And now this key to life is bent, unusable, rusted. The white racial sickness, which posits that sexuality resides in blacks, that the potency of black males must be controlled or destroyed in order for white men to gain potency, is no longer operative. In forty-two-year-old Jesse's world, blacks are no longer subject to control, and violence no longer controls them.

There is certainly no resolution to the story in the sense of what can be learned from it to inform action. It is an exposé of white American male sexuality as Baldwin sees it, and an explanation of public action based on private sickness. Even if a reader takes as less than absolutely plausible this story's explanation for the daily news coming out of the South in the mid-1960s, that reader will be struck unforgettably by the exploration of one white psyche. If the story does not satisfactorily explain collective behavior, it certainly depicts with thoroughness and plausibility what would happen in adulthood to a person hoisted onto his father's shoulders in childhood in order to see better another man quartered and burned.

"I hear music in the air":
Just Above My Head

Baldwin's most recent novel,[1] published in 1979, repeats, expands upon, and resolves many of the ideas,
questions, and conflicts that surface throughout his
published works—in interviews, debates, essays,
novels, plays, and short stories. *Just Above My Head,*
the title, is the first line of a song that Ida Scott, the
black jazz singer, sings in *Another Country:*

> Just above my head,
> I hear music in the air
> And I really do believe
> There's a God somewhere

While the novel, *Just Above My Head,* nowhere directly
states the belief of those last two song lines, in many
indirect ways there is not simply resolution in the novel,
but affirmation, even cause for joy. As elsewhere in
Baldwin's work, the joy comes only out of pain and
examination of pain. The affirmation is painstakingly
pulled out of memory. The resolution comes only out
of violent conflict.

Just Above My Head is a long novel, 597 pages in
the Dial Press edition, and is divided into five books,
the first and last the shortest, with fifty-six and sixty-
eight pages. Book One is called "Have Mercy" and is
prefaced by two epigraphs. The first, "Work: for the
night is coming," is repeated as the epigraph for Book

Three also. The second epigraph opening the novel is
from another traditional song, about the last messianic
prophet of the Old Testament.

> Daniel
>> saw the stone
> that was
>> hewed out the mountain
> Daniel
>> saw the stone
> that was
>> rolled into Babylon.
> Daniel
>> saw the stone
> that was
>> hewed out the mountain,
> tearing down
>> the kingdom of this world!

The novel proper opens with the death of "Soul
Emperor" Arthur Montana, famed gospel singer, dead
at age thirty-nine in a men's room in the basement of
a London pub. Arthur's brother, Hall, first-person narrator of the novel, describes the death, even though he
was far away in New York, awaiting Arthur's flight
from London. "The damn'd blood burst, first through
his nostrils, then pounded through the veins in his
neck, the scarlet torrent exploded through his mouth, it
reached his eyes and blinded him and brought Arthur
down, down, down, down, down."

Hall's despair at the time of the death is conveyed
with echoing repetition that demands to be read aloud.

My brother. Do you know, friend, how a brother loves his
brother, how mighty, how unanswerable it is to be confronted with the truth beneath that simple word? Simple.
Word. Yes. No. Everything becomes unanswerable, un-
readable, in the face of an event yet more unimaginable
than one's own death. It *is* one's death. . . . And do you
know, do you know, how much my brother loved me! And

do you know I did not know it? did not dare to know it:
do *you* know? No. No. No.

I looked and looked and looked at the telephone. I
looked at the telephone and I looked at the telephone.

Oh, my God my God my God my God my God, oh my
God my God my God oh no no no, my God my God my
God my God, forsake me if you will and I don't give a shit
but give me back my brother, my God my God my God
my God my God!

Then, abruptly, we move from the time of the
death to a spring Sunday two years later, the period of
Hall's narration. Hall is forty-eight years old. His father,
Paul, is dead; his mother, Florence, has returned from
New York to New Orleans. His wife, Ruth, and his
children, Tony, fifteen, and Odessa, thirteen, complete
his immediate family. Two other lifelong friends of
Hall are introduced early as well, through a dream
Hall narrates, with "me and Arthur and Jimmy and
Julia." In the dream Hall is trying to catch, then find,
Arthur, and Hall ends up in a doorway open to the sky,
"slipping off the edge, into space."

Hall's remembering Arthur's death and all that
led to it and his attempts to face the pain of it all are
spurred by a question from his son. At a gathering at
Julia's suburban New York City home, Tony expresses
his concern that famous Uncle Arthur was what Tony's
friends call a faggot. Hall tells his son that "a lot of
men . . . loved my brother. . . . I know two men—your
uncle—Arthur—loved—," one of them Julia's brother
Jimmy. But, he adds, "Whatever the fuck your uncle
was, and he was a whole lot of things, he was nobody's
faggot."

Julia recalls their earlier years and brings out
photographs and clippings. Hall, too, begins to remember, to reconstruct the past. "It takes time," Julia says,
"more time than anybody wants to imagine—to sort
things out, inside, and then try to put them together,

and then try—not so much to make *sense* out of it all
—as to *see*."

Julia was a successful Harlem child evangelist, and
an obnoxious one, from age nine to age fourteen. She
was eleven and her brother, Jimmy, was nine when
the Montana children, Arthur and Hall, first met them.
Arthur made his gospel singing debut at a Pentecost
Sunday service at which Julia preached. Arthur was
thirteen; Hall was twenty. Later Arthur sang with and
toured with a boys' quartet called The Trumpets of
Zion, and, later still, when he went solo, Hall was his
manager. Throughout, Arthur struggled not only with
his own uncertainty over his homosexual affairs, first
with another member of the quartet, Crunch, then with
Jimmy, but struggled also with what his big brother
and his parents thought. "I wouldn't be able to live,
man, if I thought you were ashamed of me," he said
to Hall.

All of these things we learn in summary form in
Book One of *Just Above My Head*. And all of these
things are developed in great detail through the rest of
the novel. "Work: for the night is coming" here tells
Hall to remember, to reconstruct, to see his past
through the mirror images of Arthur's past. "Have
Mercy" asks for time, for vision, and for courage to
retrace that past.

Book Two is called "Twelve Gates to the City."
Its epigraph is "Come on in the Lord's house: / It's
going to rain." In this book the reader has a full
view of Julia as child preacher, is given a full sermon,
in fact. The day on which Julia and Jimmy, Arthur and
Hall first meet as children is fully remembered. Each
of the members of the Trumpets of Zion quartet is introduced, and their learning to sing together, with Arthur's and Hall's father, Paul, assisting, is described,
even though Hall as narrator says, "I can't describe it, I
wasn't there."

Two years later, Christmas Eve with the four Montanas, and Christmas day with the Millers—Julia and Jimmy's parents—are developed in detail. The quartet sings, Julia preaches, and security is threatened when the serious illness of Amy Miller, Julia and Jimmy's mother, is revealed. Hall meets a bartender, Sidney, who becomes an immediate friend, and brings his girl, Martha, to the bar on Christmas night. The attempt made by the Montanas and Martha to get Amy to the hospital is foiled by young Julia, who determines rather to trust in the spirit.

During the next half year, the Trumpets of Zion leave to tour the South; Hall is drafted into service in the Korean war; Amy dies; Jimmy is sent South to his grandmother; Julia at fourteen preaches her last sermon; and Joel Miller, Julia's father, rapes her and establishes an incestuous, ongoing relationship with her. The Gates to the City are various and veiled. All the four main characters—Arthur, Hall, Jimmy, Julia— are figuratively out in a downpour at the end of Book Two. Midway through the telling of these events, Hall asks:

And what did I think, feel, I, who am trying to piece together this story, I, who am attempting to stammer out this tale? Terrified against my will, hoping to be able to face what I know I scarcely dare to face, myself in all of this, myself, and the self trapped in that brother I so righteously adored. Is adoration a blasphemy or the key to life, to life eternal, our weight in the balance of the grace of God?

Book Three, with the repeated epigraph, "Work: for the night is coming," is called "The Gospel Singer." In this book, Hall, as narrator, moves away from experiences he has direct knowledge of, into material which would have had to have been told him in great detail later by several people—by Arthur, by Crunch, by Julia. Readers are to assume, probably, that Hall's imaginative recreations are his attempt to see now what these people saw, to see from several angles in order better to understand, to see, not to "make sense" of it all.

This book is dominated by two demanding pursuits: music and love. The traveling Trumpets of Zion are followed across the mysterious, intimidating South. Arthur and Crunch, who room together, fall in love and make love, and their lovemaking gives their music an added tension, trust, and courage.

When the Trumpets return to New York, two of them to face draft notices, Crunch runs into Julia and attempts, through making love to her, to release her from the bondage to her father. Crunch leaves for Korea, telling Arthur to befriend Julia, which he does. "The Gospel Singer" is living the life he sings about in his song.

"Lead me to the rock / That is higher than I" reads the epigraph for Book Four, "Stepchild." This very long section of the novel (230 pages) covers many years in many places, opening with Hall's return from Korea and closing years later with Arthur's return from a European tour and Julia's return from a sojourn in Africa.

Racial desegregation is the national concern in the States during these years. Hall's father, upon Hall's return, tells him desegregation doesn't make much difference, "You going to have to do what we've always done, ain't nothing new—take what you have, and make what you want." Paul's mother says, "It don't mean I want to eat with white people. It just makes life a little easier—might make my children's lives a little easier." And, she adds, "we're not really talking about *them:* we talking about *us.* . . . It don't so much matter what *they* mean to do: it matters what *we* mean to do." Hall is also updated on personal changes which have taken place during his absence. Crunch made Julia pregnant, and Julia's father, Joel, beat her almost to death, aborted the baby, and then disappeared. Julia was sent to her grandmother. Sidney, Hall's friend, and Martha, his girlfriend, fell in love and became Black Muslims.

Abruptly, we move to a period five years later. Hall is returning to New York from San Francisco, where he has been working in the California branch of a New York advertising agency. It is his thirtieth birthday. On the flight east, he notices an ad with a striking black model, who proves to be Julia. He looks her up in New York, and they talk. And "somewhere between Sheridan Square and East 18th Street, Julia and I fell in love."

Julia has created a home for younger brother, Jimmy, and through Julia and Hall's affair Jimmy and Arthur, just returned from a solo Canadian tour, meet again and also fall in love but are immediately separated again by their respective tours. Jimmy plays piano at Southern civil rights rallies. "What, I had wondered," Hall says, "watching Arthur watching Jimmy, happens to the younger brother who needs a younger brother to love, and who considers that this need is forbidden?"

Despite a lengthy and happy affair with Hall, Julia suddenly leaves for the west coast of Africa, and Hall is despondent. He recovers partly through joining Arthur and Peanut, another of the former Trumpets of Zion singers, on a Southern tour. Danger is everywhere on the road and at the rallies. "Look at a map, and scare yourself half to death," Hall says. Danger culminates in the disappearance of Peanut. His body is never found. "That blow, the loss of Peanut, seemed to have the effect of fragmenting each of us where we stood, and fragmented, we scattered everywhere." Arthur goes off to tour the United States, Canada, Europe, writing postcards to Hall in "a new note—dry, wary, bitter. . . . *Love must be the rarest, most precious thing on earth, brother, where is it hiding?*" Hall moves from the white advertising agency to the ad department of a black magazine, but "I felt—unused," he says, "therefore, useless, and I felt unwanted, I felt, as the song puts it, so *unnecessary.*"

But Book Four ends on a more positive note, with a long episode of Arthur in Paris. He meets a white French insurance man, Guy Lazar, and because Arthur meets Guy's need, they seem able, in a few days and nights, to cleanse from Arthur's tortured conscience all of the pain and fear of his homosexuality, his racial, and his musical experience. Arthur and Guy use "themselves in defiance of murder, time, language, and continents, history knotted in the balls, hope, glory, and power pounding in the prick. . . ." On their final night together, they meet Sonny Carr, an old American blues singer, and Carr seems to pass on to gospel singer Arthur his blues legacy. "Arthur sings with him, the last lines of the last song they sang together that night.

> I'm pleased with what you've done,
> and your race has been run
> and I've brought you the key
> and I've got your key here with me
> and I praise God, I have another building,
> not made with hands!"

Arthur returns to New York, and Julia arrives the same day, with no one aware. The "Stepchild" in the title for Book Four may be Arthur, not quite at home in the world; it may be Peanut, lost mysteriously forever; it may be Guy Lazar, whose need gives Arthur a chance to be parent and older brother, to love, not just be loved, to be necessary. "The rock that is higher than I" has to be the power of love, taking so many forms and hues and routes.

Book Five, sixty-eight pages long, is titled "The Gates of Hell." The ominousness of that title is lessened, however, by the epigraphs: "It's me, it's me, / It's me, oh, Lord, / Standing in the need of prayer," and "I know my robe's going to fit me well / I tried it on at the gates of hell." Being at the gates of hell doesn't have to mean going in; it can mean the place for a radical turning.

Hall Montana opens Book Five with a part of his continuing narrative confession.

You have sensed my fatigue and my panic, certainly, if you have followed me until now, and you can guess how terrified I am to be approaching the end of my story. It was not meant to be my story, though it is far more my story than I would have thought, or might have wished. I have wondered, more than once, why I started it, but—I know why. It is a love song to my brother. It is an attempt to face both love and death.

It is now winter; Hall's wife and children have gone to see *The Wiz* on Broadway. Jimmy, Arthur's last and greatest love, comes over to see Hall. Jimmy and Arthur had finally gotten together after Arthur's experience with Guy and had loved and made music together for fourteen years before Arthur's death. Jimmy has expiated his guilt for the lover's quarrel that sent Arthur to London without him and led Arthur to the pub where he died, by returning to all the places they had played, to perform alone. Jimmy has come through. Hall, during those years, had met and married Ruth, had fathered two children, had managed Arthur's growing fame, had gone with him South again, and had come to understand the particular non-marrying kind of love Julia has for him, informed by her African experience. Her African lover, Julia says, "told me that I was not barren, that childbirth takes many forms, that regret is a kind of abortion, that sorrow is the only key to joy. . . . He made me be-

gin to look forward, instead of looking back. . . . I'm
learning to trust what I don't know."

Finally, Hall comes back to where he started at
the beginning of his long narrative search. "I must now
do what I have most feared to do: surrender my
brother to Jimmy, give Jimmy's piano the ultimate
solo: which must also now, be taken as the bridge."
Hall has hoped that his "hand could hold up the sky,"
that he could save Arthur from his tortured self as
from the leeches, the hangers-on who tortured Arthur.
But he couldn't hold up the sky.

Neither could Jimmy. "Arthur got hurt, trapped,
lost somewhere" in the fourteen years. "All Arthur
wanted was for the people *he* respected to respect *him*
—the people who had *made* the music. . . . It was only
when he got scared about what *they might think of
what he'd done to their song—our* song—that he really
started to be uptight about our love."

So Hall recreates Arthur's death in the pub, from
a heart attack, it appears. "He starts down the steps,
and the steps rise up, striking him in the chest again,
pounding between his shoulder blades, throwing him
down on his back, staring down at him from the ceil-
ing, just above his head."

Just Above My Head ends with another dream.
The early dream of the novel was peopled by Hall
and Arthur and Jimmy and Julia and followed the
dreamer's futile pursuit of Arthur. Hall's concluding
dream in the novel again has "Jimmy and Julia and
Arthur and me," this time "on a country porch . . .
sheltered from the rain." Florence and Paul, Sidney
and Martha, Joel and Amy are all in the rain, "trying
to help each other up the blinding road." Tony is on
Hall's shoulder; Odessa is at his knee; Ruth is at his
back. Arthur asks, twice, " 'Shall we tell them? What's
up the road?' " " 'I wish,' says Jimmy . . .'that you'd
just let the rain do whatever the rain is doing.' "

In the dream, Hall remembers the words of a song he loved to hear Arthur sing: "O, my loving brother, when the world's on fire, don't you want God's bosom to be your pillow?" And, as if in response to both questions—Shall we tell them? Don't you want God's bosom?—Hall replies, "No, they'll find out what's up the road, ain't nothing up the road but us, man."

In concept and execution, *Just Above My Head* bears resemblance to Baldwin's long short story, "Sonny's Blues." In *Tell Me How Long the Train's Been Gone* Baldwin explored the childhood and adult relationship of brothers from the younger brother's view; in "Sonny's Blues" and *Just Above My Head,* the older brother narrates the story. While the earlier novel used theater as the metaphor to convey art's relationship to life, both the short story and Baldwin's most recent novel employ music. Beyond that, both the short story and the recent novel present the younger brother as the embodiment of a mystical participation in musical art and depict the younger brother as initiating the older into understanding. Baldwin is able to expand upon these depictions in the long novel and is particularly successful at integrating gospel music into his prose and into his thematic concerns.

In "Sonny's Blues," the schoolteacher-older brother comes to some understanding of Sonny's pain and Sonny's art only when he enters Sonny's jazz-club world and listens to the music, not as "personal, private, vanishing evocations," but as art "dealing with the roar rising from the void and imposing order on it as it hits the air." At the end of Book One of *Just Above My Head,* Hall Montana recalls bar-hopping with Arthur, just before becoming his manager (both younger brothers drink Scotch and milk) and just after the birth of his son. "It was the first time I ever watched my brother in a world which was his, not mine. . . . I knew Arthur was trying to show me something, something which I might not have been able to see if I had not been drunk. Or, if Tony had not been born two nights before." The helpless, perfect baby son reminds Hall of his first sight of Arthur, tiny and furious and helpless. For the parent or the older brother to enter the world of the child, the younger, is a step into space, a step into the unknown.

Gospel lyrics and the gospel sound are to be found everywhere in *Just Above My Head*. "Maybe all gospel songs begin out of blasphemy and presumption," Hall speculates early in his narration, that is, "what the church would call blasphemy and presumption: out of entering God's suffering, and making it your own, out of entering your suffering and challenging God Almighty to have or to give or to withhold mercy."

The world enters into the music; the music enters the world. Hall's early, extended conjecture about The Trumpets of Zion members' thoughts as they sing, shows the world of adolescent sexuality entering their music.

Jesus I'll never forget man dig them oh they tell me titties man oo-ba oo-ba oh shake it off Mama an uncloudy cat's digging day you down below how did you man feel when you yeah baby keep digging come it ain't half hard yet out the wilderness oh baby! leaning don't go nowhere leaning yeah sister fox oo-ba oo-ba yeah leaning oh you precious freak you leaning on oh don't it look good to leaning you now on the Lord come on back here 'tis the old yeah and stay ship right there of Zion it going be beautiful my soul I'm going let you have looks up a little taste to Thee.

Later, Crunch and Arthur's love enters their music.

    Crunch's guitar began, as Arthur's voice began,
        Take me to the water
Crunch moaned,
        yes! take me to the water!!

He heard Red's witnessing falsetto, but he answered
Crunch's echo,

> *take me to the water*
> > *to be*
>
> *baptized.*

He paused, and closed his eyes, sweat gathered in his
hair; he listened to Crunch, then he started again,

> *Take me to the water*
> *yeah!*
> *take me to the water*
> *now!*
> *take me to the water*
> *oh, Lord!*
> *to be*
> *to be?*
> *to be*
> *tell me, now!*
> *to be*
> *to be baptized!*

He paused again, threw back his head to get the
sweat out of his eyes, trusting every second of this unprecedented darkness, knowing Crunch and he were moving together, here, now, in the song, to some new place;
they had never sung together like this before, his voice in
Crunch's sound, Crunch's sound filling his voice,

> *So*
> *I know*
> *none*
> *don't tell me, I know, I know, I know!*

Meanwhile, the music is bombarding the world.
Crunch's body is *"deep like a river"* to Arthur. In their
lovemaking,

a moment came when he felt Crunch pass from a kind of
terrified bewilderment to joy. . . . *So high, you can't get
over him.*

Sweat from Arthur's forehead fell onto Crunch's
belly.

So low—and Crunch gasped as Arthur's tongue left his
prick standing in the cold, cold air, as Arthur's tongue

licked his sacred balls—*you can't get under him.* It was as
though, with this kiss, they were forever bound together.
Crunch moaned, in absolute agony, and Arthur went down
again.
"Little fellow. Baby. Love."
You must come in at the door.

The music is in Julia's world, as her father ex-
pectantly awaits her body: "she was fourteen, and in
Ezekiel's valley, alone: *oh, Lord, can these bones
live?*" It is in her world as she tries to escape, to support herself, to rescue Jimmy: *"I got to find a way."*
It is in Hall's world as he reenters the New York City
frenzy after his Korean service, with the people celebrating homecoming—*"out of the jaws of death"*—
and the cops crying *"Keep moving. Keep moving."* It is
in Martha's world in her secure love with Sidney: *"I
once was lost, but now am found."* It is in Hall and
Julia's world as they discover each other: "So now I
can only step out, as the song says, on the promise."
And the music is everywhere in Arthur's world,
in his inability to reconcile his love with the world's
image of and treatment of that love. When

the word was out on Arthur's ass . . . lots of people tried
to gang-rape him in indescribable ways—oh, yes, believe me,
it's cold out there—and Arthur began to sink beneath the
double weight of the judgement without and the judgement
within. And, yet, it is true, and Arthur was right when he
insisted, *I've got to live the life I sing about in my song:* he
meant that he could not afford to live a lie.

The key to Blackness in this gospel music, as
Baldwin describes and depicts it, is in the "stepping
out on the promise," the anticipation, and in the beat,
and in the beat within the beat. Paul, Arthur and
Hall's pianist father, gives instruction to the Trumpets
of Zion: "The beat comes out of the *time*—the space

between one note and the next note. And you got to trust the time *you* hear—that's how you play your song." He describes music to Hall:

Music don't begin like a song. . . . Music can get to *be* a song, but it starts with a cry, that's all. It might be the cry of a newborn baby, or the sound of a hog being slaughtered, or a man when they put the knife to his balls. And that sound is everywhere. People spend their whole lives trying to drown out that sound. . . . If you ever had to think about it—how we get from sound to music—Lord, I don't know—it seems to prove to me that love is in the world—without it—music, I mean—we'd all be running around, with our fangs dripping blood.

Hall describes the Trumpets of Zion:

Niggers can sing gospel as no other people can because they aren't singing gospel. . . . When a nigger quotes the Gospel, he is not quoting: he is telling you what happened to him today, and what is certainly going to happen to you tomorrow. . . . Our suffering is our bridge to one another.

Later, Arthur tries to verbalize the difference he experienced singing with white Canadian musicians:

"I'd be up there, you know, singing, and the cats behind me would be keeping *time*—but—they couldn't—*anticipate*—you know, when you *leap* from one place to another—they couldn't be with me, I was alone—oh, brother, you've heard it all your life, like me, but I don't know how to say it—the changes some of the old church choirs could ring on 'The Old Rugged Cross,' make you hold your breath and you'd *hold* your breath until they let you know you could let it out—" he turned to me, and grinned, his hands spread wide—"you know, like Billie Holiday and Bessie Smith can just leave a note hanging somewhere while they go across town and take care of business and come back just in time and grab that note and swing out with it to someplace you had no *idea* they were going—and carry you with them, that's when you say *Amen!*"

Hall makes one of the analogies that suggest this music as the central thematic metaphor of the novel:

A stranger is a stranger is a stranger, simply, and you watch the stranger to anticipate his next move. But the people who elicit from you a depth of attention and wonder which we helplessly call love are perpetually making moves which cannot possibly be anticipated. Eventually, you realize that it never occurred to you to anticipate their next move, not only because you couldn't but because you didn't have to: it was not a question of moving on the next move, but simply, of being present.

For *Just Above My Head* is, as Hall has said, a love song to his brother, which turns out to be more about himself, and an "attempt to face both love and death." Supplementing the music as metaphor are numerous other images involving hearing and innumerable images involving eyes and seeing. The attempt to see as another sees; the attempt to see from many angles; the attempt to see in mirror images, not only in mirrors but in brothers, children, parents, and lovers; these attempts seem to underlie the narrative technique. They explain Hall's recreating whole chunks of the past which he did not see or hear directly. The title appears several times in the novel in lowered, crushing ceilings, which suggest mortality. But the music "just above my head," just beyond my vision, suggests that love and hope and trust cannot be seen or analyzed. As Hall discovers by the end of his recreating, that doesn't mean love and hope and trust are not there.

Many, many earlier Baldwin concerns reemerge in this novel, but with a difference. The social and psychological problems of homosexuality are confronted, and the homosexual and heterosexual love scenes are more direct and explicit than they were in previous works. Baldwin's many trips South, as well as his brother's trip South in the Melodeers Quartet, are effectively transformed in the sections of *Just Above My Head* dealing with civil rights efforts. Learning how to use one's individual and group past, and learning that suffering is a bridge to others, are themes appearing frequently in Baldwin's fiction, but for the first time those themes are movingly embodied in characters whose struggles are comprehensive and whose victories are believable.

The irate voice protesting against white society and against Christianity has for the most part quieted here. Instead, positive black culture and example are fully explored, and Christian convention is used to convey truth about love and living, which may, after all, *be* Christian. That is to say, Baldwin's continuing insistence that "the key to my salvation, which cannot save my body, is hidden in my flesh" (from *Giovanni's Room*) is not far distant from religion which originates in God born in human form.

There are no drastically new Baldwin themes in this novel, then, but some themes have been taken to resolution. In an interview made at the time of this last novel's publication, Baldwin said, "What I've really been feeling is that I've come full circle. From *Go Tell It on the Mountain* to *Just Above My Head* sums up something of my experience—it's difficult to articulate—that sets me free to go someplace else." [2] The circle, which is completed, and the last novel, which completes it, are like Hall's fictional search that returns to the beginning. And the optimistic note, muted but persistent, that threads its way through *Just Above My Head* suggests that Hall and Baldwin can move on to new and equally rich lodes of experience.

9

Critical Sources; Afterword

Perusing the published statements and creations of James Baldwin, the reader, with the author, comes full circle. Numerous passionate defenders of his thought and life and artistry are balanced by numerous and equally passionate detractors. Wading through vehement and sometimes shallow reactions to the deep waters of the statements and works themselves, one is struck repeatedly by the power of Baldwin's prose, and by our continuing need, as readers and as citizens, for his steadying apocalyptic vision. Finally, in his fantastic, experientially various, wide-ranging, searching, and committed life, one can find a vigorous model for venturing beyond charted areas.

Critics of Baldwin and Baldwin's work abound. His book publications, from the first, *Go Tell It on the Mountain*, 1953, to his most recent, *Just Above My Head*, 1979, have been reviewed in general readership magazines and newspapers and in professional journals. The early essay collections received more attention than the later ones, and the earlier novels received more favorable reviews, for the most part, than the later ones. Many articles on Baldwin's fiction, particularly, have been published in professional humanities journals.

Some of the best of these critical pieces have been collected and made accessible in Keneth Kinnamon,

editor, *James Baldwin: A Collection of Critical Essays*
(Englewood Cliffs, New Jersey: Prentice-Hall, Inc.,
1974); in Donald B. Gibson, editor, *Five Black Writers*
(New York: New York University Press, 1970); and in
Therman B. O'Daniel, editor, *James Baldwin: A Criti-
cal Evaluation* (Washington, D.C.: Howard University
Press, 1977).

The Kinnamon collection contains thirteen pieces,
including selections from book-length works, such as
the Baldwin chapter from Robert Bone's *The Negro
Novel in America* (1965), the chapter on the black
musician in Baldwin from Sherley Anne Williams's
Give Birth to Brightness (1972), and Eldridge Clea-
ver's notorious attack on Baldwin, "Notes on a Native
Son," from his 1968 book, *Soul on Ice*. Other articles
are from *CLA Journal, Yale Review, Literature and
Psychology, Harper's Magazine, Études Anglaises, Saturday Review*. Kinnamon includes an introductory
chapter, a chronology, and a brief bibliography, making the book a useful introduction to criticism on
Baldwin.

Gibson's *Five Black Writers* includes essays on
Richard Wright, Ralph Ellison, Langston Hughes, and
LeRoi Jones, as well as four essays on Baldwin. The
four Baldwin essays include Norman Podhoretz's "In
Defense of James Baldwin" from his book *Doings and
Undoings*, and articles from *CLA Journal* and *En-
counter*. One of the articles, John Hagopian's "James
Baldwin: The Black and the Red-White-and-Blue,"
(on the short story, "This Morning, This Evening, So
Soon"), appears in the O'Daniel anthology as well,
and another, George Kent's "Baldwin and the Problem
of Being," appears in all three collections.

Gibson's book, in addition to providing an introductory chapter comparing the five authors, and a short
bibliography for each, includes a final section of classic
essays on the subject of "The Writer and Social Re-

sponsibility." Beginning with Langston Hughes's famed 1926 manifesto, "The Negro Artist and the Racial Mountain," the section includes Baldwin's "Many Thousands Gone," his early criticism of Richard Wright, and Maurice Charney's analysis of the Baldwin-Wright quarrel. These pieces are followed by the essays that present another famous quarrel in the history of black literature, Irving Howe's "Black Boys and Native Sons," and Ralph Ellison's response in "The World and the Jug."

The third collection of critical essays on Baldwin, Therman O'Daniel's recent *James Baldwin: A Critical Evaluation,* is useful not only for reprinting articles, many of which appeared in the sometimes hard-to-find *CLA Journal,* but for printing for the first time articles on several of Baldwin's works not discussed in the other collections: *One Day, When I Was Lost, The Amen Corner, Tell Me How Long the Train's Been Gone, A Dialogue.* Articles are grouped under Baldwin as novelist (seven items); essayist (four items); short story writer (five items); playwright (three items); scenarist (one item); and "Baldwin's Raps and Dialogues" (two items). The usefulness of this collection is enhanced by a full bibliography of Baldwin's work, including his periodical pieces, and an extensive bibliography of secondary works on Baldwin.

For the reader wishing for some guidance through the plentiful secondary material published on Baldwin up to the mid-seventies, including reviews of his books, and for the reader looking for some indication of the content of Baldwin's own periodical pieces, Daryl Dance's essay in *Black American Writers: Bibliographical Essays,* Volume 2, is excellent. Entitled "James Baldwin," close to fifty pages long, published by St. Martins Press, New York, in 1978, the essay is one of several edited by M. Thomas Inge, Maurice Duke, and Jackson R. Bryer.

Dance introduces his essay by stating that, contrary to the suggestion of the title of one of Baldwin's essay collections, *Nobody Knows My Name,* "on a realistic level practically everyone knows his name, from people on the street to scholars in the most prestigious universities—and they all respond to him." This bibliographical essay, Dance continues, "considers many of these varied responses to James Baldwin, the man; James Baldwin, the spokesman for black people; James Baldwin, the essayist; and James Baldwin, the novelist." Discussion is then divided into bibliographical sources; editions of Baldwin's books; Baldwin's interviews and discussions; manuscripts and letters; biography; criticism of individual works; general studies including Baldwin; personal criticism of Baldwin; and future needs in Baldwin criticism. There are a few errors in the citations, and some article summaries are misleading, but for the most part the essay is an extremely useful and readable way to get an overall picture of primary and secondary material on Baldwin.

A much lengthier and more thorough, but less readable, way to survey work on Baldwin is through the 1980 publication by Fred Standley and Nancy Standley, *James Baldwin: A Reference Guide* (G. K. Hall: Boston, 1980). The authors' preface describes the listing of secondary sources on Baldwin and his work as "a chronological, annotated survey of reviews, commentaries and interpretations about his works as well as its containing significant references to him found in books, periodicals, newspapers, monographs, and dissertations both in English and in several foreign languages." Works on Baldwin are alphabetized, from 1953 to a partial listing for 1978. The annotations, many of them quite lengthy, are written with a combination of quote and paraphrase. An index includes not only authors, titles of works, names of people, but thirty-nine subject areas such as "sex," "homosexuality," "civil rights spokesman," "violence," "movies," "love." Finally, the Standley and Standley *Reference Guide* contains an initial listing of writings by Baldwin, divided first into "Books" and "Other Works." The latter are divided into "Essays, Reviews, Letters"; "Dialogues, Debates, Discussions"; "Short Stories, Excerpts"; "Interviews"; and "Recordings, Films." Within each of these categories, the works are arranged alphabetically.

There are not many book-length studies of Baldwin as yet. Stanley Macebuh's *James Baldwin: A Critical Study* (New York: Third Press-Joseph Okpaku, 1973) looks mostly at the novels to that date. Fern Eckman's *The Furious Passage of James Baldwin* (1966) is biographical, based on interviews with Baldwin. It includes much information available nowhere else. Louis H. Pratt's *James Baldwin*, in Twayne's United States Authors Series (Boston: G. K. Hall, 1978), reads like the dissertation it is based on, but is thorough and is useful in providing short annotations for secondary sources. William Weatherby's *Squaring Off: Mailer Vs. Baldwin* (New York: Charter, 1977) is a readable, intriguing book by a British journalist, friend of both Baldwin and author Norman Mailer. The book enables the reader to see Baldwin in the context of socially-engaged writing beyond the race question.

Of two book-length studies by European critics, Karin Möller's *The Theme of Identity in the Essays of James Baldwin* (Göteborg, Sweden: Acta Universitatis Gotoburgensis, 1975), one of the Gothenburg Studies in English Series, is in English. As a study concentrating on Baldwin's essays, Möller's work is unique, difficult, insightful. Another study, by German critic Peter Bruck, is in German, but Bruck provides a full English summary of his main points in an appendix. *Von der "Storefront Church" zum "Ameri-*

can Dream": James Baldwin und der amerikanische Rassenkonflikt was published in Amsterdam by Verlag B. R. Grüner in 1975.

Several doctoral dissertations have been done on Baldwin. Helen Ruth Houston's annotations on dissertations in *The Afro-American Novel 1965–1975: A Descriptive Bibliography of Primary and Secondary Material* (Troy, New York: Whitston, 1977) are very helpful in surveying work done in dissertation form. *Dissertation Abstracts International* of course includes full and frequently useful abstracts of dissertations. Houston's bibliography on Baldwin covering the 1965–1975 period includes some seventy-five annotated items. Just as there is no shortage of material in print by Baldwin, there is no shortage, either, of material about him and his work, and no shortage of guides to that material.

What can one say after summarizing, sampling, analyzing and interpreting the work of James Baldwin and reactions to that work, except that here is a writer of exceptional range and power. What is sometimes lacking in aesthetic control over long art forms such as the novel is more than adequately made up for by concisely constructed scenes, descriptions, sentences. Some of Baldwin's habits are bound to be irritating to some readers—his use of profanity, his explicit and sentimental sex scenes, his castigation of white America, his seeming inability to rid himself of early religious training he finds bothersome but ingrained, his repetition of some ideas, phrases, scenes. But what emerges, nevertheless, from the whole of his work, is a kind of absolute conviction and passion and honesty that is nothing less than courageous.

When his work is joined with his life, the picture of courage grows. As we see Baldwin now victorious against the odds of poverty, race, stature, looks, homosexuality, publishing realities for black authors, it is needful to remind ourselves of the struggle that victory represents. We must remind ourselves because Baldwin has shared his struggle with his readers for a purpose—to demonstrate that our suffering is our bridge to one another. For an introduction to his life and work to do less than state that ultimate purpose behind everything Baldwin has written would be, I think, to do him a disservice.

Recently Baldwin said, "I think the whole concept of race has had its day. . . . Ultimately, to be white is a moral choice." [1] Baldwin is, ultimately, not talking and writing about skin color at all, but about pain, commitment, about seeing and hearing, about honesty in relation to one's past, one's present, and one's future as a person and as a people. His own honest witness—"I was there"—is meaningful only if readers hear it and act on it.

Again, in a recent interview, Baldwin summed up his *raison d'etre.* It is appropriate to give him the final solo, which is, as with Jimmy's narration in *Just Above My Head,* also the bridge, the connecting passage between the writer and the reader.

You write in order to change the world, knowing perfectly well that you probably can't, but also knowing that literature is indispensable to the world. In some way, your aspirations and concern for a single man in fact do begin to change the world. The world changes according to the way people see it, and if you alter, even by a millimeter, the way a person looks or people look at reality, then you can change it.[2]

Notes

1

1. James Baldwin's nonfiction is clearly the kind of autobiographical writing that Robert Sayre describes in "The Proper Study—Autobiographies in American Studies," *American Quarterly,* XXIX (1977), 241–262, as including particularly for contemporary black writers open letters, preachments, apology, parable or representative anecdote, the capitulatory brief, the tirade, the narrative or polemical expose, the public prayer, appeal to conscience, call to arms. "Not to recognize these as sometimes the most important forms of autobiography would be like throwing away half the tools (and weapons) of survival," he says.
2. James Baldwin, "Interview with Inmates at Riker's Island Prison in New York," *Essence,* June, 1976, p. 55.
3. James Baldwin, "Disturber of the Peace," with E. Auchincloss and N. Lynch, *Mademoiselle,* May 1963, p. 204.
4. Baldwin, "Interview . . .," p. 80
5. James Baldwin, "Notes of a Native Son," *Notes of a Native Son* (New York: Bantam, 1955), p. 71.
6. Ibid., p. 95.
7. James Baldwin, "Negroes are Anti-Semitic Because They're Anti-White," *New York Times Magazine,* 9 April 1967, p. 27.
8. James Baldwin, Margaret Mead, *A Rap on Race* (Philadelphia: Lippincott, 1971), p. 206.

9. "Conversation: Ida Lewis and James Baldwin," *Essence,* October 1970, pp. 25–26.
10. Baldwin, "Disturber . . .," p. 205.
11. Baldwin, Mead, p. 39.
12. James Baldwin, "Bright World Darkened," *New Leader,* 24 January 1948, p. 11; and "Autobiographical Notes," *Notes of a Native Son* (New York: Bantam, 1955), p. 2.
13. William J. Weatherby, *Squaring Off: Mailer Vs. Baldwin* (New York: Mason Charter, 1977), p. 83.
14. Ibid., p. 14.
15. James Baldwin talks with Kenneth Clark," *The Negro Protest* (Boston: Beacon Press, 1963), pp. 6–7.
16. Weatherby, p. 24.
17. Baldwin, "Autobiographical Notes," p. 1; "Interview . . . ," p. 55.
18. Ibid., p. 55
19. Ibid.
20. James Baldwin, "The Black Boy Looks at the White Boy," *Nobody Knows My Name* (New York: Dial Press, 1961), p. 233.
21. James Baldwin, *The Devil Finds Work* (New York: Dial Press, 1976), p. 32.
22. James Baldwin, "East River Downtown: Postscript to a Letter from Harlem," *Nobody Knows My Name* (New York: Dial Press, 1961), p. 81.
23. James Baldwin, "Autobiographical Notes," p. 2.
24. James Baldwin, *No Name in the Street* (New York: Dial Press, 1972), p. 23.
25. James Baldwin, "The New Lost Generation," *Esquire,* July 1961, p. 113.
26. Ibid., p. 114.
27. James Baldwin, Nikki Giovanni, *A Dialogue* (Philadelphia: Lippincott, 1973), pp. 14–15.
28. James Baldwin, "Alas, Poor Richard," *Nobody Knows My Name* (New York: Dial Press, 1961), pp. 188–89.
29. Weatherby, p. 84.
30. James Baldwin, "There's a Bill Due that Has to Be Paid," *Life,* May 1963, p. 81.

31. Weatherby, pp. 89–90. Baldwin's 1961 essay, "The Black Boy Looks at the White Boy," first published in *Esquire* and collected in *Nobody Knows My Name,* thirteen essays reprinted in 1961, gives Baldwin's view of his relationship to Mailer. Baldwin describes himself at their first meeting in 1956 in Paris as "a very tight, tense, lean, abnormally ambitious, abnormally intelligent, and hungry black cat."

32. Ibid., pp. 99, 138.

33. James Baldwin, "To Whom It May Concern: A Report from Occupied Territory," *The Nation,* 11 July 1966, p. 41; "How Can We Get the Black People to Cool It?" *Esquire,* July 1968, pp. 49, 53.

34. James Baldwin, "The Nigger We Invent," *Integrated Education* (March/April, 1969), p. 20

35. Baldwin, *No Name in the Street.*

36. "Conversation . . .," p. 24.

37. Weatherby, p. 197.

38. Robert Cole, "James Baldwin Back Home," *New York Times Book Review,* 31 July 1977, p. 22.

39. James Baldwin, "As Much Truth As One Can Bear," *New York Times Book Review,* 14 January 1962, p. 38.

40. "The Black Scholar Interviews James Baldwin," *Black Scholar,* 5, iv (1973–1974), pp. 40, 41.

41. Sally Smith, "James Baldwin: The Expatriate Becomes Disillusioned," *Atlanta Constitution,* 19 May 1976, p. 21. Quoted by Louis H. Pratt, *James Baldwin* (Boston: Twayne Publishers, 1978), p. 28.

2

1. James Baldwin, "Lockridge: the American Myth," *New Leader,* 10 April 1948, p. 10.

2. James Baldwin, "History as Nightmare," *New Leader,* 25 October 1947, p. 11.

3. M. Preston, ed., "The Image: Three Views," *Opera News,* 8 December 1962, p. 10.

4. James Baldwin, "Creative Dilemma," *Saturday Review,* 8 February 1964, p. 58.

5. James Baldwin, "Down at the Cross: A Letter from a Region in My Mind," *The Fire Next Time* (New York: Dell, 1964), p. 111.

6. James Baldwin with Richard Avedon, *Nothing Personal* (New York: Atheneum, 1964), n.p.

7. James Baldwin, "In Search of a Majority: An Address," *Nobody Knows My Name* (New York: Dial, 1961), p. 134.

8. Baldwin, "Down at the Cross . . . ," p. 35.

9. James Baldwin, "Autobiographical Notes," *Notes of a Native Son* (Boston: Beacon Press, 1955), p. 4.

10. James Baldwin, "The Negro in American Culture," *Cross Currents* (Summer, 1961), p. 205.

11. James Baldwin, "A Talk to Teachers," *Saturday Review,* 21 December 1963, p. 44.

12. James Baldwin, "Disturber of the Peace," with E. Auchincloss and W. Lynch, *Mademoiselle,* May 1963, p. 202.

13. James Baldwin, "History of Nightmare," *New Leader,* 25 October 1947, p. 11.

14. James Baldwin, "Everybody's Protest Novel," *Notes of a Native Son* (Boston: Beacon Press, 1955), pp. 15–16.

15. James Baldwin, "What Price Freedom?" *Freedomways,* Spring 1964, p. 191.

16. James Baldwin, "Fifth Avenue, Uptown: A Letter from Harlem," *Nobody Knows My Name* (New York: Dial, 1961), p. 71.

17. James Baldwin, "Stranger in the Village," *Notes of a Native Son* (Boston: Beacon Press, 1955), p. 149.

18. James Baldwin with Nikki Giovanni, *A Dialogue* (Philadelphia: Lippincott, 1973), p. 74.

19. Baldwin, "What Price Freedom?" p. 193.

20. James Baldwin and William F. Buckley, Jr., (Debate) "The American Dream and the American Negro," *New York Times Magazine,* 7 March 1965, p. 88.

21. Baldwin, "Disturber . . . ," p. 202.

22. James Baldwin, "My Dungeon Shook: Letter to My Nephew on the One Hundredth Anniversary of the

Emancipation," *The Fire Next Time* (New York: Dell, 1964), p. 21.

23. James Baldwin, "How Can We Get the Black People to Cool It?" *Esquire,* July 1968, p. 51.

24. "The Black Scholar Interviews James Baldwin," *Black Scholar,* 5 (1973–1974), 34–35.

25. James Baldwin, "Faulkner and Desegregation," *Nobody Knows My Name* (New York: Dial, 1961), p. 117.

26. James Baldwin, "Letters from a Journey," *Harper's,* May 1963, p. 49.

27. James Baldwin, Nathan Glazer, Sidney Hook, Gunner Myrdal, "Liberalism and the Negro: A Round-table Discussion," *Commentary,* March 1964, p. 35.

28. James Baldwin, "Crusade of Indignation," *The Nation,* 7 July 1956, p. 19.

29. Baldwin, "How Can We Get . . .," p. 53

30. James Baldwin with Joe Walker, "Exclusive Interview with James Baldwin," *Muhammad Speaks,* 6 October 1972, p. 31.

31. Baldwin, "Autobiographical Notes," p. 6.

32. Baldwin, Walker, p. 30.

33. James Baldwin, "As Much Truth as One Can Bear," *New York Times Book Review,* 14 January, 1962, p. 38.

34. Baldwin, "The Negro in American Culture," p. 206.

35. Baldwin, Walker, 8 September 1972, p. 14.

36. "Conversation: Ida Lewis and James Baldwin," *Essence,* October 1970, p. 27.

37. James Baldwin with Margaret Mead, *A Rap on Race* (Philadelphia: Lippincott, 1971), p. 201.

38. James Baldwin, "Interview with Inmates at Riker's Island Prison in New York," *Essence* (June, 1976), p. 55.

39. Baldwin, "My Dungeon Shook . . . ," p. 19.

40. James Baldwin, *No Name in the Street* (New York: Dial, 1972), p. 23.

41. Baldwin, "Autobiographical Notes," p. 6.

42. James Baldwin, James Mossman, and Colin Mac-

Innes, "Race, Hate, Sex and Colour; A Conversation," *Encounter,* July 1965, p. 56.

43. Baldwin, Giovanni, p. 94.

44. James Baldwin, "Literary Grab Bag," *New Leader,* 28 February 1949, p. 11.

45. James Baldwin, "Modern Rover Boys," *New Leader,* 14 August 1948, p. 12.

46. James Baldwin, "The New Lost Generation," *Esquire,* July 1961, p. 115.

47. James Baldwin, "The Northern Protestant," *Nobody Knows My Name* (New York: Dial, 1961), p. 179.

48. James Baldwin, "The Black Boy Looks at the White Boy," *Nobody Knows My Name* (New York: Dial, 1961), p. 227.

49. Baldwin, "The Northern . . . ," p. 166.

50. James Baldwin, "The Dangerous Road Before Martin Luther King," *Harper's,* February 1961, p. 33.

51. Baldwin, "My Dungeon Shook . . . ," p. 18.

52. James Baldwin, "Mass Culture and the Creative Artist: Some Personal Notes," *Daedalus,* Spring 1960, p. 375.

53. For example, "The Precarious Vogue of Ingmar Bergman," *Esquire,* April 1960, pp. 128–132, collected as "The Northern Protestant," *Nobody Knows My Name;* "The Black Boy Looks at the White Boy," *Esquire,* May 1961, collected under the same title with slight revisions also in *Nobody Knows My Name.*

54. "Equal in Paris," *Notes of a Native Son* (Boston: Beacon Press, 1955), pp. 134, 129.

55. Robert Sayre, "The Proper Study—Autobiographies in American Studies," *American Quarterly,* 1977, p. 257.

3

1. James Baldwin, *Go Tell It on the Mountain* (New York: Dell, 1963). All quotations from the novel will be taken from the Dell paperback.

2. Michel Fabre, "Fathers and Sons in James Baldwin's *Go Tell It on the Mountain,*" in *James Baldwin: A Collection of Critical Essays,* ed. Keneth Kinnamon (Englewood Cliffs, New Jersey: Prentice-Hall, Inc., 1974), p. 120. Fabre's essay was first published in French in *Études Anglaises,* 23, no. 1 (1970), 47–61.

3. John Hope Franklin, *From Slavery to Freedom* (New York: Knopf, 1974), pp. 349, 415, 356–57.

4. Robert Bone, "James Baldwin," in *James Baldwin: A Collection of Critical Essays,* ed. Keneth Kinnamon (Englewood Cliffs, New Jersey: Prentice-Hall, Inc., 1974), p. 36. Bone's essay is part of his *Negro Novel in America,* rev. ed. (New Haven: Yale University Press, 1965).

5. Fabre, pp. 136–37.

4

1. James Baldwin, *Giovanni's Room* (New York: Dell, 1956), and *Another Country* (New York: Dell, 1960). All references to these novels will be to these editions.

2. See, for example, James Baldwin and Richard Avedon, *Nothing Personal* (New York: Atheneum, 1964). See also Chapter Two.

5

1. James Baldwin, *Tell Me How Long the Train's Been Gone* (New York: Dell, 1968). All references to the novel are from this edition.

2. See Daryl Dance, "James Baldwin," in *Black American Writers: Bibliographical Essays,* Vol. 2, ed. M. Thomas Inge, Maurice Duke, Jackson Bryer (New York: St. Martin's Press, 1978), pp. 102–103, for a summary of critical reaction. "Errant association" is the term used by William Edward Farrison in "If Baldwin's

Train Has Not Gone," in *James Baldwin: A Critical Evaluation,* ed. Therman B. O'Daniel (Washington, D.C.: Howard University Press, 1977), to describe the way the story is developed—"the connection between the various episodes is left for the reader to discover or supply for himself" (p. 71). Farrison is also vehemently critical of Baldwin's vulgar language.

3. James Baldwin, *If Beale Street Could Talk* (New York: New American Library, 1974). All references to the novel are from this edition.

4. See Jacqueline E. Orsagh, "Baldwin's Female Characters: A Step Forward?" in O'Daniel, ed., *James Baldwin: A Critical Evaluation,* pp. 56–68, for a very good discussion of strong female characters in Baldwin's novels.

5. James Baldwin, with Herbert R. Lottman, "It's Hard to Be James Baldwin," *Intellectual Digest,* July 1972, p. 68.

6. Ibid.

7. Ibid., pp. 67–68; and W. J. Weatherby, *Squaring Off: Mailer vs Baldwin* (New York: Mason/Charter, 1977), pp. 212–213.

6

1. James Baldwin, *The Amen Corner* (London: Michael Joseph, 1968), p. 14. All references to the play will be to this edition.

2. James Baldwin, "Theatre: The Negro In and Out," *Negro Digest,* April 1966, p. 41.

3. Carlton W. Molette, "James Baldwin as a Playwright," in *James Baldwin: A Critical Evaluation,* ed. Therman B. O'Daniel (Washington, D.C.: Howard University Press, 1977), pp. 183, 188.

4. Ibid., p. 184.

5. Darwin T. Turner, "James Baldwin in the Dilemma of the Black Dramatist," in *James Baldwin: A Critical Evaluation,* p. 194.

6.   James Baldwin, *Blues for Mister Charlie* (New York: Dell, 1964). All references to the play will be from this edition. Many of the scenes and events that appear in *Blues for Mister Charlie* are developed from Baldwin's own experiences traveling in the South. A 1961 essay, for example, "The Dangerous Road Before Martin Luther King," in *Harper's,* describes King's church in Montgomery, Alabama as directly across from "a white, domed building. . . . The conjunction of the two buildings, the steepled one low and dark and tense, the domed one higher and dead white and forbidding, sums up, with an explicitness a set designer might hesitate to copy, the struggle now going on in Montgomery."

7.   Baldwin expressed a similar concern much earlier, also, in a 1949 essay, "Preservation of Innocence," in *Zero.* "And what of murder?" Baldwin wrote then. "A human characteristic, surely. Must we embrace the murderer? But the question must be put another way: is it possible not to embrace him? For he is in us and of us. We may not be free until we understand him."

8.   Turner, pp. 191, 192.

9.   Molette, pp. 186–87.

10. James Baldwin, *One Day, When I Was Lost: A Scenario Based on Alex Haley's "The Autobiography of Malcolm X"* (New York: Dial Press, 1973). All references to the scenario are from this edition.

11. Patsy Bremington Perry, "One Day, When I Was Lost: Baldwin's Unfulfilled Obligation," in *James Baldwin: A Critical Evaluation*, pp. 213–227.

12. The dramatic version of *Giovanni's Room* has not been considered in this chapter since it is not available in print.

7

1.   *Black American Writers: Bibliographical Essays,* ed. M. Thomas Inge, Maurice Duke, and Jackson R. Bryer

(New York: St. Martin's Press, 1978). In addition to Baldwin, Volume 2 covers Richard Wright, Ralph El-lison, and Amiri Baraka (Leroi Jones).

2. See Sam Bluefarb's discussion of the story in "James Baldwin's 'Previous Condition': A Problem of Identi-fication," in *Five Black Writers,* ed. Donald Gibson (New York: New York University Press, 1970), and in *James Baldwin: A Critical Evaluation,* ed. Therman B. O'Daniel (Washington, D.C.: Howard University Press, 1977). Bluefarb's article appeared originally in *Negro American Literature Forum.*

3. John M. Reilly, " 'Sonny's Blues': James Baldwin's Im-age of Black Community," in *Five Black Writers* and *James Baldwin: A Critical Evaluation.* The article first appeared in *Negro American Literature Forum.*

4. An edited and annotated edition of "This Morning, This Evening, So Soon," has been published by Johan-nes Schütze (Frankfurt an Main: Verlag Moritz Die-sterweg, 1968). The annotations are primarily for non-American readers and include translations of colloquial and slang expressions and explanations of allusions.

5. John V. Hagopian, "James Baldwin: The Black and the Red-White-and-Blue," in *Five Black Writers,* pp. 159–60. The article originally appeared in *CLA Jour-nal* and is reprinted also in *James Baldwin: A Critical Evaluation.*

6. Ibid., p. 163.

7. See Arthemia Bates Millican, "Fire as the Symbol of a Leadening Existence in 'Going to Meet the Man,' " in *James Baldwin: A Critical Evaluation.*

8

1. James Baldwin, *Just Above My Head* (New York: Dial Press, 1979). References to the novel are from this edi-tion. Parts of *Just Above My Head* were published in Penthouse in 1978.

2. James Baldwin (Interview with Mel Watkins), "James

Baldwin Writing and Talking," *New York Times Book Review*, 23 September 1979, p. 3.

9

1. "James Baldwin Writing and Talking," an interview with Mel Watkins, *New York Times Book Review*, 23 September 1979, p. 36.
2. Ibid., p. 37.

Bibliography

WORKS BY JAMES BALDWIN

Books

Go Tell It on the Mountain. New York: Alfred A. Knopf, 1953.

Notes of a Native Son. Boston: Beacon Press, 1955.

Giovanni's Room. New York: Dial Press, 1956.

Nobody Knows My Name: More Notes of a Native Son. New York: Dial Press, 1961.

Another Country. New York: Dial Press, 1962.

The Fire Next Time. New York: Dial Press, 1963.

Blues for Mister Charlie. New York: Dial Press, 1964.

Nothing Personal. Photographs by Richard Avedon and text by James Baldwin. New York: Atheneum Publishers, 1964.

Going to Meet the Man. New York: Dial Press, 1965.

The Amen Corner. New York: Dial Press, 1968.

Tell Me How Long the Train's Been Gone. New York: Dial Press, 1968.

A Rap on Race. By Margaret Mead and James Baldwin. Philadelphia: J. B. Lippincott Company, 1971.

No Name in the Street. New York: Dial Press, 1972.

One Day, When I Was Lost: A Scenario Based on Alex Haley's "The Autobiography of Malcolm X." New York: Dial Press, 1973.

A Dialogue. By James Baldwin and Nikki Giovanni. Philadelphia: J. B. Lippincott Company, 1973.

If Beale Street Could Talk. New York: Dial Press, 1974.

The Devil Finds Work: An Essay. New York: Dial Press, 1976.

Little Man, Little Man: A Story of Childhood. Illustrated by Yoren Cazac. New York: Dial Press, 1976.

Just Above My Head. New York: Dial Press, 1979.

Book Reviews, Articles, Interviews, Discussions

Reprinting in Baldwin collection of essays and short stories is indicated. (Reprinting in other collections is *not* indicated.)

"When the War Hit Brownsville." *New Leader,* 17 May 1947, p. 12.

"Smaller than Life." *Nation,* 19 July 1947, pp. 78–79.

"Without Grisly Gaiety." *New Leader,* 20 September 1947, p. 12

"History as Nightmare." *New Leader,* 25 October 1947, pp. 11, 15.

"Battle Hymn." *New Leader,* 29 November 1947, p. 10.

"Dead Hand of Caldwell." *New Leader,* 6 December 1947, p. 10.

"Maxim Gorki as Artist." *Nation,* 12 April 1947, pp. 427–428.

"Bright World Darkened." *New Leader,* 24 January 1948, p. 11.

"Literary Grab Bag." *New Leader,* 28 February 1948, p. 11.

"The Harlem Ghetto: Winter 1948." *Commentary,* February 1948, pp. 165–170. In *Notes of a Native Son.*

"Present and Future." *New Leader,* 13 March 1948, p. 11.

"Lockridge: 'The American Myth.' " *New Leader,* 10 April 1948, pp. 10, 14.

"Change Within a Channel." *New Leader,* 24 April 1948, p. 11.

"Modern Rover Boys." *New Leader,* 14 August 1948, p. 12.

"Previous Condition." *Commentary,* October 1948, pp. 334–42. In *Going to Meet the Man.*

"Journey to Atlanta." *The New Leader,* 9 October 1948, pp. 8–9. In *Notes of a Native Son.*

"The Image of the Negro." *Commentary,* April 1948, pp. 378–80.

"Everybody's Protest Novel." *Zero* (France), Spring 1949, pp. 54–58. In *Notes of a Native Son*.

"Preservation of Innocence." *Zero* (Morocco), Summer 1949, pp. 14–22.

"Too Late, Too Late." *Commentary*, January 1949, pp. 96–99.

"Death of the Prophet: A Story." *Commentary*, March 1950, pp. 257–261.

"The Negro in Paris." *Reporter*, 6 June 1950, pp. 34–36. In *Notes of a Native Son* as "Encounter on the Seine: Black Meets Brown."

"The Outing." *New Story* No. 2 (1951), pp. 52–81. In *Going to Meet the Man*.

"The Negro at Home and Abroad." *Reporter*, 27 November 1951, pp. 36–37.

"Many Thousands Gone." *Partisan Review*, November–December, 1951, pp. 665–80. In *Notes of a Native Son*.

"Exodus." *American Mercury*, August 1952, pp. 97–103. Incorporated in *Go Tell It on the Mountain*.

"Roy's Wound." *New World Writing*, November 1952, pp. 109–116. Incorporated in *Go Tell It on the Mountain*.

"Stranger in the Village." *Harper's*, October 1953, pp. 42–48. In *Notes of a Native Son*.

"The Amen Corner." *Zero*, July 1954, pp. 4–8, 11–13. Act I of *The Amen Corner*.

"A Question of Identity." *Partisan Review*, July–August 1954, pp. 402–10. In *Notes of a Native Son*.

"Gide as Husband and Homosexual." *The New Leader*, 13 December 1954, pp. 18–20. In *Nobody Knows My Name* as "The Male Prison."

"Life Straight in De Eye." *Commentary*, January 1955, pp. 74–77. In *Notes of a Native Son* as "Carmen Jones: The Dark is Light Enough."

"Equal in Paris." *Commentary*, March 1955, pp. 251–59. In *Notes of a Native Son*.

"Me and My House." *Harper's*, November 1955, pp. 54–61. In *Notes of a Native Son* as "Notes of a Native Son."

"The Crusade of Indignation." *Nation*, 7 July 1956, pp. 18–22.

"Faulkner and Desegregation." *Partisan Review*, Fall 1956, pp. 568–73. In *Nobody Knows My Name*.

"Princes and Powers." *Encounter*, January 1957, pp. 52–60. In *Nobody Knows My Name*.

"Sonny's Blues." *Partisan Review*, Summer 1957, pp. 327–58. In *Going to Meet the Man*.

"Come Out of the Wilderness." *Mademoiselle*, March 1958, p. 102. In *Going to Meet the Man*.

"The Hard Kind of Courage." *Harper's*, October 1958, pp. 61–65. In *Nobody Knows My Name* as "A Fly in the Buttermilk."

"The Discovery of What It Means to Be an American." *New York Times Book Review*, 25 January 1959, pp. 4, 22. In *Nobody Knows My Name*.

"Sermons and Blues." *New York Times Book Review*, 29 March 1959, p. 6.

"On Catfish Row: *Porgy and Bess* in the Movies." *Commentary*, September 1959, pp. 246–48.

"Letter from the South: Nobody Knows My Name." *Partisan Review*, Winter 1959, pp. 72–82. In *Nobody Knows My Name* as "Nobody Knows My Name: Letter from the South."

"A Word From the Writer Directly to Reader." *Fiction of the Fifties: A Decade of American Writing*. Ed. Herbert Gold. Garden City, N.Y.: Doubleday, 1959, pp. 18–19.

"Any Day Now." *Partisan Review*, Spring 1960, pp. 282–94. Incorporated in *Another Country*.

"Mass Culture and the Creative Artist: Some Personal Notes." *Daedalus*, Spring 1960, pp. 373–76.

"The Precarious Vogue of Ingmar Bergman." *Esquire*, April 1960, pp. 128–32. In *Nobody Knows My Name* as "The Northern Protestant."

"Fifth Avenue, Uptown: A Letter From Harlem." *Esquire*, July 1960, pp. 70–76. In *Nobody Knows My Name*.

"They Can't Turn Back." *Mademoiselle*, August 1960, pp. 324–25; 351–58.

"This Morning, This Evening, So Soon." *Atlantic Monthly*, September 1960, pp. 34–52. In *Going to Meet the Man*.

"Notes for a Hypothetical Novel." An address delivered at the Third Annual *Esquire* Magazine Symposium on "The Role of the Writer in America" at San Francisco State College, 2 October 1960. In *Nobody Knows My Name.*

"Among the Recent Letters to the Editor." *New York Times Book Review,* 26 February 1961, pp. 52–53.

"The Dangerous Road Before Martin Luther King." *Harper's,* February 1961, pp. 33–42.

"A Negro Assays the Negro Mood." *New York Times Magazine,* 12 March 1961, pp. 25, 103–104. In *Nobody Knows My Name* as "East River Downtown: Postscript to a Letter From Harlem."

"The Survival of Richard Wright." *The Reporter,* 16 March 1961, pp. 52–55. In *Nobody Knows My Name* as "Eight Men."

"Richard Wright." *Encounter,* April 1961, pp. 53–60. In *Nobody Knows My Name* as "The Exile."

"The Black Boy Looks at the White Boy" (Norman Mailer). *Esquire,* May 1961, pp. 102–106. In *Nobody Knows My Name.*

"The New Lost Generation." *Esquire,* July 1961, pp. 113–15.

"The Negro in American Culture." *Cross Currents,* Summer 1961, pp. 205–224.

In *Nationalism, Colonialism and the United States, One Minute to Twelve, A Forum.* New York: Liberation Committee for Africa, 1961, pp. 23–27.

"An Interview." *WMFT Perspective,* December 1961, p. 37.

"As Much Truth as One Can Bear." *New York Times Book Review,* 14 January 1962, pp. 1, 38.

"Letter From a Region in My Mind." *New Yorker,* 17 November 1962, pp. 59–144. In *The Fire Next Time* as "Down at the Cross: Letter From a Region in My Mind."

"A Letter to My Nephew." *Progressive,* December 1962, pp. 19–20. In *The Fire Next Time* as "My Dungeon Shook: Letter to My Nephew on the One Hundredth Anniversary of the Emancipation."

"What's the Reason Why: A Symposium by Best Selling Authors." *New York Times Book Review,* 2 December 1962, p. 3.

"Color." *Esquire,* December 1962, pp. 225, 252.

"The Image: Three Views." Symposium. Ed. M. Preston. *Opera News,* 8 December 1962, pp. 8–12.

"Easy Rider." *The Dial: An Annual of Fiction.* New York: Dial, 1962. Incorporated in *Another Country.*

"My Childhood." (Film). Metropolitan Broadcasting Television. Benchmark Films, 1962.

"The Artist's Struggle for Identity." *Liberation,* March 1963, pp. 9–11.

"Disturber of the Peace." Interview by E. Auchincloss and N. Lynch. *Mademoiselle,* May 1963, pp. 174–75, 199–207.

"There's a Bill Due That Has to Be Paid." *Life,* 24 May 1963, pp. 81–84.

"Letters from a Journey." *Harper's,* May 1963, pp. 48–52.

Black Man in America. (Recorded: Interview with Studs Terkel). Distributed by Credo, Cambridge, Massachusetts. Discussed by John Ciardi in *Saturday Review,* 6 July 1963, p. 13.

"We Can Change the Country." *Liberation,* October 1963, pp. 7–8.

"James Baldwin Talks with Kenneth Clark." *The Negro Protest.* Ed. Kenneth Clark. Boston: Beacon, 1963, pp. 4–14.

"A Talk to Teachers." *Saturday Review,* 21 December 1963, pp. 42–44; 60.

"Creative Dilemma." *Saturday Review,* 8 February 1964, pp. 14–15; 58.

"What Price Freedom?" *Freedomways,* Spring 1964, pp. 191–95. Speech to SNCC Conference on Food and Freedom.

"Liberalism and the Negro: A Round-Table Discussion." By James Baldwin, Nathan Glazer, Sidney Hooks, and Gunnar Myrdal. *Commentary,* March 1964, pp. 25–42.

"The American Dream and the American Negro." By James Baldwin and William F. Buckley, Jr. [Transcript of debate, slightly condensed]. *New York Times Magazine,* 7 March 1965, pp. 32–33; 87–89.

"What Kind of Men Cry?" [James Baldwin, Harry Belafonte, Sidney Poitier, and other men give their views]. *Ebony,* June 1965, p. 47.

"Race, Hate, Sex, and Colour: A Conversation." By James Baldwin with James Mossman and Colin MacInnes. *Encounter,* July 1965, pp. 55–60.

"The White Man's Guilt." *Ebony,* August 1965, pp. 47–48.

"Theatre: The Negro In and Out." *Negro Digest,* April 1966, pp. 37–44.

"To Whom It May Concern: A Report from Occupied Territory." *Nation,* 11 July 1966, pp. 39–43.

"Tell Me How Long the Train's Been Gone." *McCall's,* February 1967, pp. 118–19, 154, 156, 158–60, 162, 164, 166.

"James Baldwin Breaks His Silence: An Interview." *Atlas,* March 1967, pp. 47–49.

"Negroes Are Anti-Semitic Because They Are Anti-White." *New York Times Magazine,* 9 April 1967, pp. 26–27; 135–40.

"The War Crimes Tribunal." *Freedomways,* Summer 1967, pp. 242–44.

"Giovanni's Room and Another Country." Record. CMS Records, 1967. Descriptive notes on slipcase.

"*Go Tell It on the Mountain;* Excerpt." *Wilson Library Bulletin* 42 (June 1968), pp. 984–85.

"How Can We Get the Black People to Cool It? An Interview with James Baldwin." *Esquire,* July 1968, pp. 49–53; 116.

"Sidney Poitier." *Look,* 23 July 1968, p. 50.

"White Racism or World Community?" *Ecumenical Review,* October 1968. Address to World Council of Churches in Uppsala, Sweden.

"Unnameable Objects, Unspeakable Crimes." In *Black on Black: Commentaries by Negro Americans.* Ed. Arnold Adoff. New York: Macmillan, 1968, pp. 105–113.

"The Nigger We Invent." *Integrated Education,* March/April 1969, pp. 15–23. Testimony to House Select Subcommittee on Labor to establish a National Commission on Negro History and Culture.

"From Dreams of Love to Dreams of Terror." In *Natural Enemies? Youth and the Clash of Generations.* Ed. Alexander Klein. Philadelphia: Lippincott, 1969.

"Sweet Lorraine." *Esquire,* November 1969, pp. 139–40.

"Are We on the Edge of a Civil War?" Interview with David Frost. In *The Americans,* David Frost. New York: Stein and Day, 1970, pp. 145–150.

"A Rap On Race." By Margaret Mead and James Baldwin. [Excerpts]. *McCall's,* June 1971, p. 84.

"Malcolm and Martin." *Esquire,* April 1972, p. 94.

"It's Hard to Be James Baldwin." Interview with Herbert R. Lottman. *Intellectual Digest,* July 1972, pp. 67–68.

" 'Let Me Finish, let me finish . . .': A Television Conversation." By James Baldwin with Peregrine Worsthorne and Bryan Magee (Chairman). *Encounter,* September 1972, pp. 27–33.

"Exclusive Interview with James Baldwin." Joe Walker. *Muhammad Speaks,* September 8, 15, 29; October 6, 1973, pp. 13–14; 29; 29–30; 30–31.

Interview, Dick Cavett Show. (Unpublished). (5 September 1973).

"The Black Scholar Interviews James Baldwin." *Black Scholar,* 5, iv (1973–1974), pp. 33–42.

"Interview with Inmates at Riker's Island Prison in New York." Ed. Jewell Handy Gresham. *Essence,* June 1976, pp. 55, 80, 82, 85–6.

"Roots: The Saga of an American Family by Alex Haley (a Review)." *New York Times Book Review,* 26 September 1976, pp. 1–2.

"James Baldwin Writing and Talking." Interview by Mel Watkins. *New York Times Book Review,* 23 September 1979, pp. 3; 35–36.

COLLECTIONS OF AND GUIDES TO WORKS
ABOUT BALDWIN

Fischer, Russell G. "James Baldwin: A Bibliography, 1947–
      1962." *Bulletin of Bibliography*, January–April 1965.
Jones, Mary E. "James Baldwin." *CAAS Bibliography*, Num-
      ber 5 (Center for African and African-American Stud-
      ies, Atlanta University).
Kindt, Kathleen. "James Baldwin: A Checklist: 1947–1962."
      Bulletin of Bibliography, January–April 1965.
Standley, Fred L. "James Baldwin: A Checklist: 1963–
      1967." *Bulletin of Bibliography*, August 1968.

See also the works discussed in the section on critical sources
in Chapter 9.

Index

MODERN LITERATURE SERIES

In the same series (continued from page ii)